'Divine Ins

By

Mary Hession

Inspirational poetry by Mary Hession

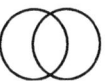

Inner Sanctum

*To Chastin
with love & blessings
from Mary x*

'Divine Inspirations'
By
Mary Hession

© 2004 Mary Hession

ISBN 0-9542421-5-7

Full publishing rights held by
'Inner Sanctum Publications'

This publication may not be altered, or changed, or sold,
or used commercially in any way.

Cover design by Mary Hession
Using artwork entitled 'L'Innocence' by William Adolphe
Bouguereau 1825-1905

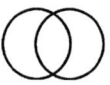

Inner Sanctum Publications

Contents & Credits

There is no structured content to this book. It can be read from cover to cover in the normal fashion, or it can be opened at random, whenever and wherever you so choose.

Mary Hession holds full copyright on all of the poetry in this book. Please do not use without first obtaining her permission to do so. Permission for use is usually granted, providing full credit is given to Mary for her compositions. Mary can be contacted via 'Inner Sanctum Publications'.

Many of Mary's poems have been set to music, illustrated in beautiful backgrounds and are available to send as e-cards. To find out more about Mary's music, songs and poetry, visit the web sites below:

'Divine Inspirations'
Inspirational poetry, midi music and songs,
by Mary Hession, for all to freely share.
http://www.maryhession.clara.net

And

'Gaia Books and Music'
Words and music to nourish your soul
http://www.gaiabooksandmusic.com

A Few Words from Mary

I honour all races, all colours, all creeds, for there are many paths, which all eventually lead to the same destination, but there is only one way and that is **THE WAY OF LOVE**.

It matters not what name we use to pray, for there is only **ONE GOD** who is known by many different names **GOD IS LOVE and LOVE IS GOD.**

Neither does it matter whether we refer to God as being He or She, for in truth He and/or She is neither and also both, for God is an energy, not a person, an energy of **PURE UNCONDITIONAL LOVE.**

My God is **LOVE** and **NATURE** is my church and I thank God for the numerous gifts and blessings that He/She has bestowed upon me in great abundance.

Amongst the many are ~ the gift of music ~ the gift of poetry ~ the gift of Love ~ and the gift of Life itself.

In eternal love and gratitude, I dedicate my life, my music and my poetry to our Heavenly Father/Mother God ~ The Divine Creative Source of All that Is.

The Holy Spirit inspires me and flows like a great river through all of my compositions. They are musical and poetic interpretations, of the living presence of God in all things.

May all who journey through these pages, be blessed by The Divine Light, in the Purity of God's Eternal Love.

Mary

Come With Me on a Journey

Come with me on a journey
A journey in riddles and rhyme
Down a mystical path of enchantment
Where there is no such thing as time

We'll laugh and we'll dance in the flowers
Meet fairies along the way
I'll show you the key to eternity
And with radiant angels we'll pray

All that you need is a heart that's pure
And love is the way that you choose
You'll honour all of Creation
With love and with joy you'll enthuse

So if you meet all the requirements
And would like to learn more as we go
Just follow me closely and listen
To you divine worlds I will show

***

Sacred Song

His sweet pure Love is all I know
Held in His arms pure gold I glow
I hear His voice and time stands still
His Holy Word my soul doth fill

His song I sing out loud in praise
The hearts and souls of man to raise
His name I honour in sacred song
The message heard in every tongue

Celebrating Life

Running round in circles
Seeking here and there
Looking for life's purpose
Its secret yearn to share

Endless one-way streets
Going nowhere fast
Searching for the answer
None better than the last

Time has come to stop now
Cease and be at rest
The power you are seeking
Is neither East nor West

No need to travel endless miles
No need to roam at all
Your purpose lies within you
It's buried in your soul

So close your eyes and go within
And seek your inner self
That is where the answer lies
A fountain of such wealth

The way you seek is simply Love
The source of all that is
Love is the answer to all things
Embrace it with a kiss

And then you'll change the pattern
From circles round and round
And journey on intended path
A spiral now is found

Sweet mystery of life is Love
So simple yet so true
You need no other teacher than
The love that lives in you

***

Truth

Pagan Christian Buddhist all
Side by side do follow the call

The paths to truth are many and long
With joy in your heart sing love's sweet song

No matter what name you use to pray
It matters not for one glorious day

We'll all meet together in radiance bright
And bathe in the source of all knowledge and Light

So let not your minds tear you apart
Think only of love and act from the heart

***

Paradise Lost

Paradise lost can be paradise found
All you have to do is to follow the sound
Of your own inner voice that whispers within
That sings in your soul deep down within

The song is of love and eternal sweet bliss
Born of our Father and Mother God's kiss
For God be both male and female too
The two merge as One and are born in the two

Pure love and pure wisdom Creator Divine
Goddess and God in pure love entwine
Man in their image was intended to be
Droplets divine in love's endless sea

When man remembers his essence divine
And returns to love's river and follows the sign
Paradise lost will once more be found
As the fountain of life resonates sacred sound

***

Sacred Dance

My spirit full on nectar sweet
In Love Divine its fruit I eat
Nought can compare this food Divine
My soul doth swim in sacred wine

Floating in Love's pure bliss
His lips on mine in sacred kiss
My heart and soul and spirit reel
In sacred dance His Love I feel

Pool of Light

Step into my pool of Light
Bathe in living waters bright
Wash away the ties of earth
To life anew give wondrous birth

My sun doth shine and wait for you
My water's wait to cleanse you too
The breath of life awaits your soul
Pure gentle Earth will make thee whole

So place yourself upon the shore
And call to Me and ask for more
Pure of spirit now's the time
I call to thee in sound and rhyme

***

Waves of Sound

Waves of sound lap Etheric shores
Flowing gently from The Source
Caressing each and every soul
Its peaceful rhythm doth console

Ebbing and flowing in rhythmic trance
Cascading pure love in divine dance
Pulsating with life it knows no bounds
Beneath the sea ripples sacred sounds

***

Reflections on the Seasons

In nature many truths are found
Open your eyes and look around
Truths are there for all to see
Mysteries shared on breath of She

Sleeping waking sleeping waking
In breaths out breaths She is taking
Like the river ever flowing
The way of life to you is showing

Look into Her heart and know
Truths unveiled to you She'll show
Reflections in the water showing
Inner eyes have inner knowing

The water flows on to the sea
To be reborn in womb of She
New life comes forth from Her once more
Birthed in love on divine shore

And so the season's come and goes
Natural law in ebb and flow
There is no death just eternal life
From Father God and Sacred Wife

For God both male and female be
Two halves of One in divine sea
When Father Mother merge as One
From Sacred Seed explodes new Sun

***

Deep Within

Deep within your soul doth lie
Memories of times gone by
They slumber soft till you awake
Then venture forth new path to take

Close your eyes and ask yourself
What be this sacred inner wealth
Then be still and listen to
The knowingness that is of you

The Light of Love doth flicker low
Awaiting time when it will grow
To beam so bright fanned by She
Who calls to thee and holds the key

To golden door that beckons you
See it now come into view
Will you enter in once more?
And let thy waiting spirit soar

Ponder on these words I write
And read them with your inner sight
Nectar sweet for you doth wait
Along the path through golden gate

As was as is eternity
For those who walk in Light of He
Guardian pure will show the way
Where all do dwell in gold array

***

A Prayer for Peace

Heavenly Father Creator Divine
With love in our hearts we pray
Enfold our beautiful Mother The Earth
In Thy Love and Light this day

No matter what colour or race or creed
We are all Thy children on this planet earth
May love touch all hearts as we sing in one tongue
For peace to be brought unto birth

Please help every soul to find their own peace
For love and peace start with self
To bring forth that peace and share it with love
Which will manifest spiritual wealth

Guide each one of our steps to find our own God
The name that we use matters not
For Love is Thy real name ~ yes God means Pure Love
Anything other than love, of Thee it is not!

***

The above prayer for peace was written for International Day of Peace
21st September 2003

Oh Ancient Land of Palestine

Oh ancient land of Palestine
Where sacred feet did tread
Remember how he showed the way
'tis love sweet love he said

Why does no one listen now?
The God of Love they shun
They bite the hand that feeds them
And shoot it with a gun

Know they not they kill themselves
For all that we give out
Returns to us in magnitude
Of that there is no doubt

Christians Jews Muslims all
It matters not the name
The only way to find your God
Is love for all the same

Jesus taught the way of love
Mr Gandhi too
Buddha he did teach the same
Mohammed also too

They all taught love thy neighbour
They all knew love's the way
It matters not which name you use
'tis to One God all pray

***

Waves of Love

From the beginning of time there was you and I
Creator Divine
Pure Love of mine
Merging as One in the waters of life
Consort Divine
Sacred Wife
We ebb and we flow in the waves of Pure Love
Blessing all life as sweet waters do flow
Love's pure bliss
Eternal sweet kiss
An ocean of Light making love to the shore
I am the water
I am the land
Lifting
Falling
Waves of delight
From Love all things flow
To Love they return
There is no beginning
Nor is there an end
For Love is forever
One moment divine

***

The Spiral of Life

In nature many truths are found
Open your hearts and look around
A constant cycle of rebirth
Eternal life of Mother Earth

No death just sleep to rest a while
And then She wakens with a smile
In robes a new Her spirit born
From long dark night to bright new dawn

To live again in pastures new
The spiral of life for all to view
The same for us we come we go
Round and round as we do grow

From infant years of pure new spring
Through summertime in joy we sing
And into autumn journey on
To winter's sleep where we are one

To rest a while before rebirth
To wondrous life on Mother Earth
Round and round we go again
Eternity in great Amen

***

Love Is

Love Is the beginning and the end
And all things in between

Love Is Creation in manifestation
Seen and unseen

Love Is the source of all that is
And is to be

Love Is the river of life that cleanses body and spirit
An endless divine sea

Love Is the breath of life that nourishes heart and soul
The eternal breath of The Creator Divine

Love Is the fire of life that warms and nurtures
And in radiance and joy doth shine

Love Is the womb of the earth
From whom all life is born as sacred waters flow

Love Is all there is
And in the fragrance of spirit doth shine and glow

***

The Heart of God

Reflections on the gift of life
I look and see around
Abundant gifts of Mother Earth
Everywhere are found

Butterflies so delicate
Pretty wings that glow
Daffodils so pure and bright
Dance and sing hello

The fragrance of the flowers
The songs of all the birds
Majestic trees and mountains
Their beauty defies words

The heart of God is open
Wide for all to see
Be still and watch and listen
Take time out just to be

***

Spirals of Light

Constantly moving spiralling high
Like clusters of stars bright in the sky
Forever reaching towards The Source
Inwardly knowing following our course

Dancing turning pulsating with light
Expanding growing shining so bright
Returning in love from whence we came
In love we do honour His Holy Name

Walking in Gold

Walking in gold on sacred ground
Whispers of Love all around
Man was placed as custodians here
To live in joy and love not fear

To tend to the trees and watch them grow
New seeds of life to also sow
The animals too and birds of the air
Were created in love for all to share

The joy of life is a precious gift
Abundance for all our spirits to lift
For those that seek and follow the sign
Will live in wondrous Love Divine

The latter days that were foretold
Are finally here for all to behold
Now's the time to make your choice
For or against Love's pure sweet voice

Those against will perish and die
And those for Love in joy will fly
For Love doth give the gift of life
Without it all will fade in strife

It's up to you the choice is yours
Follow the path through golden doors
To live in joy and Love as One
'neath golden rays of radiant Sun

***

Bouquet of Thoughts

A bouquet of thoughts from the garden of my mind
Sent with much love to all of mankind
Thoughts of peace of joy and of love
Delivered on wings of pure Holy Dove

A time of rejoicing for gifts now bestowed
Our Earthly Mother once more doth unfold
Abundance galore for all men to share
The fruits of Her love nought else can compare

Her cycle now enters the autumn of life
With a harvest divine from our Father's pure wife
In joy She doth feed us pure food from Her breast
Before Her time comes to slumber and rest

So send thoughts of love to our Mother The Earth
And thank Her for all that She brings unto birth
Tell Her you love Her and show that you care
Return all Her love in a moment of prayer

***

The Love of Souls

The love of souls beyond compare
In endless bliss entwined they share
Forever One eternally
In timelessness sweet ecstasy

No thoughts of past or future be
Immersed as One love's endless sea
Infinity in love's embrace
Sweet gift of God in Divine Grace

Womb

Tumbling from the womb of Earth
Cascading water's bring to birth
A current flowing strong and true
Surging forth on path anew

A righteous power its course is set
Within itself its purpose met
Nought will stop the path She takes
Roaring down Her way She makes

Stopping not She carries on
Eternal spring from womb of One
From The Source of all that Is
Her water's break the earth is kissed

To Herself She doth return
Through barren rocks that cry and yearn
For food of life they reach and crave
Oh save us from an early grave

Touch us with Thy waters pure
Open us that we might soar
From dessert sand where soon shall bloom
New shoots of life that sing love's tune

Then all shall bathe in Love Divine
And know each other by the sign
Know these things and be aware
With you the words of God I share

***

Without Love

Without Love the spirit cries
Without Love the spirit dies
Love is all the spirit needs
On its nectar sweet it feeds

Love is life and all there is
Love sweet love doth bring such bliss
Come and bathe in waters pure
Float in Love forever more

Without Love the spirit cries
Without Love the spirit dies
Love is all the spirit needs
On its nectar sweet it feeds

Take a sip of sacred wine
That flows freely from the vine
Fill thy soul with Love Divine
In its radiance you will shine

Without Love the spirit cries
Without Love the spirit dies
Love is all the spirit needs
On its nectar sweet it feeds

***

Let Peace Be in Your Heart

Let peace be in your heart
For of the One we are all a part
No matter what colour or race or creed
We come from One Source The Divine Sacred Seed

Let Love flow from one to another
Father and mother, sister and brother
The animals too and birds of the air
In love were all made, in love should all share

The oceans and seas and trees growing tall
In love were created, in love to us call
Please care for us know us and treat us with love
Let us all live together in peace and in love

***

Allah and God

Allah and God are One and the same
The only difference is in the name
They both mean Pure Love Creator Divine
So look not to the name, but the Light that doth shine

Allah and God feed on love not on war
Allah is God who is Allah for sure
Paths there are many, the way it is love
To the same destination where all is Pure Love

***

Morning Delights

Morning delights a gift from above
I greet gentle birds and my pure white dove
Created by God a joy to behold
Such precious companions bring forth love untold

On wings of love they come unto me
Trusting and knowing that safe they will be
They feed from my table free from all harm
Feeling Love's presence they land on my arm

This is how 'twas intended to be
That man honour nature and let birds fly free
Birds were meant to fly free in the air
To live 'longside man and in pure love to share

So take not their freedom or cause any pain
Honour all life and respect all the same
God doth give life and abundance galore
Give love to His creatures and your soul will soar

***

Holy Spirit

Such Love I feel when You are near
You fill my soul when You appear
I see Thy form my spirit soars
In Love my soul and spirit Yours

Your eyes meet mine in joy do greet
Thy Holy Spirit my soul doth meet
You lift me high above all things
To fly in Love on golden wings

Under the Ocean

Under the ocean abundance is found
Millions of life forms swimming around
A world of their own wondrous to see
How nature intended vibrant and free

Fish weren't intended to live in glass bowls
Caged up by man who imprisons their souls
God gave all freedom to roam as they please
And fish were created to swim in the seas

All creatures were given their own special place
To share life with man in wisdom and grace
So care for God's creatures don't cause any pain
Allow them their freedom if you want the same

For whatever we do doth rebound on us tenfold
If you give out pure love you'll receive love untold
So live life with love and joy in your heart
And know that of God we're all each a part

***

Wishing Pool

Look down deep within her soul
Angel of Water will make thee whole
Ask that she cleanse and purify you
Then drink of her water let it flow right through you

The power of pure water has magical gifts
It cleanses your body and your spirit it lifts
Washing away all that's not pure
Preparing the way to a mystical door

When you have bathed in her essence divine
Like droplets of water you also will shine
Then make a wish that she will unfold
The secrets of heaven for your heart to hold

With joy she will teach you and take you to meet
Her sisters of air and of sun you will greet
Sun Air and Water will help you rebirth
Your soul and your spirit in gentle pure Earth

***

Infinity

Mother Earth born of Love
Her consort Holy Pure White Dove
Together in Love's pure delight
Re-create in dark of night

Love sweet Love is all they know
In joy and bliss they both do glow
Lifting falling waves of Love
Sweet rhapsody unending Love

Eternal cycle round and round
Universal cosmic sound
No past or future now alone
Infinity in Love is known

***

May Peace Prevail Upon This Earth

May peace prevail upon this earth
Let seeds of Light be brought to birth
From darkest night they now awake
To greet the dawn and rainbows make

Nourished by sweet gentle rain
From Gaia's womb where they have lain
Awaiting warmth of golden sun
Emerging now becoming One

Reaching out in purest love
'neath outstretched wings of Holy Dove
Let pain and suffering be no more
Let Love rain down extinguish war

The power of Love doth reign supreme
Like Phoenix from the ashes seen
All nations join now hand in hand
In love one heart one earth one land

***

Heaven Is My Father's Love

Heaven is my Father's Love
His Holy Spirit Holy Dove
By my side where're I go
Such bliss untold in Him I glow

The cares of earth just disappear
When in my heart His voice I hear
I feel His presence all around
I praise His name in words and sound

Nought can compare the Love I feel
My heart and soul and spirit reel
In pure delight His essence seeing
In Him I live and have my being

***

The Cycle of Life

The cycle of life is all around
Everywhere you look it's found
Mother Nature holds the key
And shows to us how things be

There is no death just constant rebirth
The in breath and out breath of Mother Earth
She breathes out life in abundance galore
Then breathes it back to recycle once more

We come and we go in this glorious plan
The truth found in nature is same also for man
Our Earthly Mother looks after our needs
In love and abundance our bodies She feeds

And when day is done and we slumber once more
Our Heavenly Father doth open His door
He greets us with Love in His spirit we shine
As we rest in Pure Love of Creator Divine

***

Mists of Time

In the mists of time that flows
A vibrant land where nature grows
Pastures green and waters deep
Beside the temple gates do sweep

And in the temple gardens fine
Hidden in the mists of time
Wondrous flowers of every hue
Fragrant in the morning dew

Where creatures roam as they do please
Immersed in love and at their ease
Living side by side with man
As was laid down within the plan

Birds of the air do come and go
Such beauteous colours they do show
And others walk among the trees
Filled with butterflies and bees

A land where love is everywhere
Its sweet aroma fills the air
A land which is to be reborn
And soon once more one glorious dawn

Will live again in wondrous hue
As golden days come into view
Where all will share in love's sweet song
And sing its tune the whole day long

A temple new now quietly waits
For gentle ones to find its gates
Be still and hear its bells do chime
Beckoning from the mists of time

The Way of Love

The way of Love is ancient and pure
And guides the way to heaven's door
Be not afraid follow and see
Where all that is, is of Me

Put your trust in Love and know
All you seek to you I'll show
Riches of spirit beyond compare
For pure of heart in Love to share

Call My name and seek The Way
And if in purity you pray
Angel being's will show the way
On rainbow wings in dazzling array

Hold on tight unto My Word
Each and every call is heard
But only those sincere and pure
Will enter through Love's golden door

***

Eternal Friends

Guardian angel brother friend
These words for you with love are penned
Always with me at my side
My every thought in you confide

Thank you for your Light so bright
And joy that gives my heart delight
Sacred brother teacher friend
Eternal Love to you I send

The Long Night of the Soul

The long night of the soul
I've been there who has not
But when you're going through it
Pleasant it is not

You feel you're all alone
That no one understands
Confusion reigns at every turn
Whilst sinking in quick sands

People say do this
People say do that
They all have different answers
And they've got them all off pat

No one else can help you
Though they all mean well
It's you yourself that truly knows
How to save yourself from hell

So stop listening to the others
Listen to your inner self
The truth lies deep within you
A fountain of such wealth

Ask yourself what's wrong here
You know the answer well
But do not be afraid to admit it
And then your truth to tell

It matters not what other's think
Be true unto thyself
Forget material values
And look to spiritual wealth

It's your spirit that's not happy
It's suffocating fast
It needs to breathe and fly away
Before its fate is cast

***

The Breath of God

The breath of God gave life to Earth
The breath of God in Divine Birth
The breath of God birthed all living things
The breath of God on angel's wings

He breathed the oceans and the seas
He breathed the mountains and the trees
He breathed the creatures living there
He breathed it all that we might share

In all His wondrous gifts divine
That all should know Him by the sign
And live in joy and purest Love
And touch His spirit Holy Dove

Sweet breath of God please breathe on me
Sweet breath of God please help me see
Sweet breath of God so gentle pure
Sweet breath of God in Thee I soar

***

Sacred Cargo

Mary and Ruth for France did set sail
Carrying with them the Holy Grail
A vessel yes, but not of the earth
The womb of God prepared soon for birth

Their journey protected shrouded in mist
A rainbow above them in Etheric pure kiss
Hidden away from those who sought harm
Their vessel did sail upon waters made calm

Their journey complete in France they did land
Guided each step by unseen Divine Hand
Daughters of Light two made of one
Did carry the seed of His Beloved Son

In a cave their home they did make
And wait for the day when they would awake
To glorious moment long since foretold
Of children of Light cloaked all in gold

Two as one both born of He
Pure Holy Bloodline of sacred tree
Hidden and safe in the arms of Pure Love
Watched over protected by His Holy Dove

They grew in the knowledge and laws of old
The secret arts to them were told
The ways of the Priestess with Consort Divine
Acknowledged revered throughout mists of time

And when they were grown and had learnt all things well
They left on their journeys the world then to tell
To carry the teachings and sow their own seed
The Gospel of Light to a world much in need

And so of today it is still much the same
Their spirit's live on and still teach in His name
Their forms are now different but the spirits within
Are just as they were in Divine Light of Him

***

Love Rains Down

Rain falls down from heaven
Awash with Love Divine
In its wondrous sparkle
Neons of Light do shine

Rippling jewels of Light
Aglow with seeds of Love
Infiltrating darkness
Nurtured from above

Raise your eyes look up now
A sign for all to see
In purest waters falling
No end of Love on thee

Reborn in Living Waters
Awake from dark of night
Inhale sweet breath of morning
Now see God's sunlight bright

Raise yourself above the dark
Arise on golden beams
In riddle and rhyme much truth is found
Nothing is all that it seems

***

Forest Brook

The forest brook flows to the sea
Its path assured strong and free
Determined sure its way it makes
It twists and winds its journey takes

No dam can stop its powerful course
It flows in radiance from its source
Dazzling sparkling shining bright
Surging on with all its might

Its destiny is known in full
From tiny stream doth ocean pull
Unto itself to be reborn
In waters pure sweet love adorn

***

Solitude

Now both are gone I am alone
Devoid of earthly ties
In Love I give myself to Thee
In Love my spirit flies

The chains of sadness fall away
Leaving bonds of love
You are my life my life is yours
My radiant Holy Dove

I dress myself in robes of white
I place my hands in Thine
With You I share Eternal Bliss
In wondrous Love Divine

The things of earth are transient
They pass are quickly gone
The Love of God is infinite
In You in Love I'm One

***

Sacred River

Sacred River sparkling with Light
Flowing with life dazzling and bright
Bathe in her water so cleansing and pure
Swim soft and gentle through open gold door

Cascading fountains shimmer within
Rainbows of Light dance twirl and spin
Creating beauty and glowing with Light
Like golden stars radiant at night

Refreshed and renewed in waters pure
Time to return through bright gold door
Back on the shore look back and see
She whispers and sighs and flows on to the sea

***

Rising Out Of Chaos

God is both God and Goddess too
Both become One merged in the two

In divine sacred union with Holy Pure Dove
The trinity is complete in Unconditional Pure Love

Born from the union all life doth flow
In radiance divine and wondrous glow

Divine cosmic dance in waters divine
The in breath and out breath with rainbows doth shine

Sparkling jewels of heavenly light
Cascading in brilliant celestial light

When man comes to realise that he too can shine
Making spirals of light that are also divine

This world will be lifted from long dark black night
And shine like a beacon in radiant pure light

***

Dance of Joy

A dance of joy in love's sweet bliss
Divine embrace eternal kiss
To the stars around the moon
In sunlight bright the earth doth swoon

Goddess divine in sacred dance
Doth sing in joy in love's sweet trance
Sister daughter mother wife
Spiral in the dance of life

Rainbows of light cascade and twirl
Sweet waters flow in wondrous swirl
Time stands still all is reborn
And angels sing this glorious dawn

***

Healing Dreams

Rest and let your body heal
In arms of love embraced
Dream of love, in nature walk
Her healing balm now taste

Golden kisses on thy lips
Fresh breeze upon your face
Butterflies and flowers greet
Your spirit dressed in lace

Sleep sweet child of gentle earth
And let thy spirit soar
To fly in golden realms in joy
Where all is love so pure

Return renewed from slumber deep
Your health now growing strong
Awake unto still in thine ear
Sweet echoes of love's song

***

Mothers Love

A mother's love is powerful and strong
Yet soft and gentle too
It comes from deep within the soul
I share it now with you

These words do pour forth from my heart
Cascading love to all
It matters not your colour or creed
My love I give to all

Every day is 'Mother's Day'
With love given and received
From Mother Nature all were born
In Love of God conceived

For God both Father Mother be
In sacredness divine
And from the nurturing feminine side
Goddess divine doth shine

So take this love now offered
And feel it with your heart
And feel Pure Unconditional Love
Of which we're all a part

For God doth love all nations
And God doth love all creeds
With Love Divine our Mother God
Her children nectar feeds

***

On Wings Of Love

Sacred brother my best friend
With love to you these words are penned
Always with me by my side
In you my deepest thoughts confide

I hear your voice within my heart
Of me you'll always be a part
My hands in thine we travel far
On wings of love to furthest star

We live in joy in love's delight
A shining beacon in the night
You know my needs without a word
In silent bliss your voice is heard

We merge as One in still of night
Creating Light cascading bright
That all might hear the sacred sound
Of Love that echoes round and round

***

Bliss Untold

Bliss untold I know with Thee
Thy Holy Spirit flows through me
Past and present future meet
Eternally as one they greet

Thy name in joy my spirit sings
My soul takes flight on golden wings
It soars to heaven up above
And flies as One with Holy Dove

We Are What We Eat

We are what we eat this is so true
Whatever you eat becomes a part of you
To eat animals killed just for man's greed
Is not what your body needs to feed

Consume death and you hasten the death of yourself
Eat living food enriched with health
Eat fruits of the earth, nuts grains and seeds
Your body will thank you as on life it feeds

Death brings forth death and life brings forth life
These words were once spoken by Jesus The Christ
Most of his teachings were hidden away
But finally now will see light of day

He honoured Our Mother, Our Mother The Earth
From Her life is given as She brings to birth
All manner of fruits on Her table She lays
Enough to feed all through all of our days

So think just before you take your next bite
Will this do me good and fill me with Light
For God's Light is borne in all living things
Rejoice in the gifts that Divine Mother brings

***

Sunset Waters

The longest day doth kiss the night
And stretch in bliss and pure delight
A dance of joy twixt earth and sky
Gaia's song is heard on high

Sun and moon in rhapsody
Embrace in love's eternal sea
Join them now in celebration
Of all the wonders of Creation

See the beauty in the skies
Such majesty doth bring such sighs
Eternity in cosmic dance
Sun Earth and Moon in divine trance

And so we celebrate the Light
In warmth and joy of sunlight bright
Three in one and one in three
As was as is forever be

(Written for the Summer Solstice)

***

Reflections of Autumn

Reflections of autumn a joy to behold
Our beautiful Mother's all clothed in gold
Crimson burnt orange a feast for the eyes
Adorned in such beauty in radiance She lies

A carpet of wonder doth kiss velvet green
Creation divine in such majesty seen
Breathe in Her beauty and nourish your soul
Bathe in Her essence and She'll make thee whole

Warmed by Her love your spirit will glow
Delights of Creation to you She doth show
For the heart of our God Creator Divine
In Her doth abide and in radiance they shine

Through My Eyes

Through my eyes I see the beauty of Creation
Through my eyes I see the beauty of each nation
Through my eyes I see the beauty in all creeds
Through my eyes I see the love each soul needs

Through my eyes shines The Light of The Mother
Through my eyes shines The Light of my Brother
Through my eyes shines The Light of The Sun
Through my eyes shines The Light of The One

Through my eyes flows the Divine Fountain
Through my eyes shimmers the Sacred Mountain
Through my eyes burns The Eternal Flame
Through my eyes whispers Love's Holy Name

Through my eyes I sing the song of The Dove
Through my eyes I beckon to those of Pure Love
Through my eyes I silently call unto thee
Through my eyes I send Love to set all souls free

***

Love Is Life

Life is love, love is life
It lifts above all human strife
Eternal food of love so pure
Waits for you through golden door

Meet in Love with gentle Earth
Give your spirit divine birth
Find the temple enter in
Bathe in Light that flows from Him

Born in Love the spirit flies
In radiance bright in azure skies
In to the stars that glow above
It soars in Love with Pure White Dove

***

Make Love Not War

Make love not war it's the only way
And do it now our God doth say
Turn the tide before it's too late
And save our world from dismal fate

A part of God each one are we
Meant to share in love's pure sea
Made in God's image male and female are
Merge both in love and create divine flower

For God is both masculine and feminine too
A droplet divine lives in each one of you
Blend two halves as one in radiance divine
Make rainbows so bright that glisten and shine

Like crystals and jewels of wonder and awe
Two spirits as one in great joy will then soar
Up to the stars and back unto earth
In joy and in love gentle earth will rebirth

***

As Nature Intended

Living foods are given free
In great abundance born of She
Goddess pure provides our needs
With love and life our bodies feeds

Fruits of trees and fruits of earth
All our bodies need to birth
A way of life that's wholesome pure
And was intended that's for sure

Living food brings life and health
Filled with nature's vibrant wealth
Created by The Divine Hand
Born in Love from natural land

Eat what Mother Earth provides
Free from harm and pesticides
Leave alone the sprays of man
They're not a part of Divine Plan

Greed of man has caused such harm
Illness pain and much alarm
Toxic poisons everywhere
In food and water and in the air

Detox your life as best you can
Live close to nature not to man
Live in love with natural law
And let your mind and spirit soar

Our Father God and Mother Earth
In Love as One do bring to birth
All that we do ever need
From Divine table take their seed

The Wonder Of It All

Wondrous sights I see all around
Butterflies bright and bees are found
Pretty flowers filled with light
Shimmering in the morning light

Fragile yet strong made of love
All sent from heaven up above
Dancing around on gossamer wings
With joy and love how my heart sings

Oh how I love sweet nature's delights
Pure joy and bliss such precious sites
Sounds of bird songs fill the air
Nought else on earth can compare

My spirit glows just to see
All of God's wonder in a tree
Flowers and creatures everywhere
Such fragrance divine doth fill the air

Thank you my God for all that I see
Thank you for sharing them with me
Gifts divine true treasures of earth
From Gaia's womb in sacred birth

Mother Divine born of sweet Love
Blessed in the heavens up above
Birthing all life in constant rebirth
My heart is filled with joy and mirth

***

Seeds Of Change

Seeds of change in the wind do blow
I hear their song and in my heart I know
Expectation fills the air
A time to love a time to share

The hand of God doth touch my soul
Be true to Me I'll make thee whole
When all else fades withers and dies
My Love is constant within you it lies

Hold on tight to the spirit within
It will not fail you and soon you'll begin
To forge a new path to horizons new
And know that My Love is always with you

Let go of all past sadness and pain
Detach and let go soon it will wane
And into a bright new tomorrow you'll glide
My Spirit is always close by your side

***

Eternal Flame

I Am The Eternal Flame
I bless all those who call My name
The waters of life I give to thee
Drink and set your spirits free

The food of life is Pure Love
Brought on wings of Radiant Dove
Seek within the temple gates
Golden table quietly waits

For spirits pure there's nectar sweet
Come and find thy waiting seat
Where all is Love and purity
Where all that is, is of Me

***

My Guardian Angel

Guardian angel by my side
All my thoughts in you confide
You have watched me through the years
Through pain and joy and smiles and tears

I love you so my special friend
When things go wrong your love doth mend
And lift me high once more to swim
In endless love that flows from Him

Your radiant smile and sparkling eyes
Please me so and bring such sighs
Of love so pure of love so deep
My eyes with tears of joy do weep

With me since before I was
Eternal friends we are because
Our spirit's harmonise in Love
That flows through us from Holy Dove

We share His Love in purity
That flows through you that flows through me
I pray that we may always be
Together in Love's endless sea

***

Heaven Sent

When the world lets you down
And there's no one seems to care

When you feel all alone
And there's no one there to share

Your sadness and pain that hurt so much
And all that you long for is a tender loving touch

Just turn to that special person and say
Please come to me and by my side please lay

Put your hand in mine let me feel you so near
Fold your arms around me and let me hear

Your gentle sweet breath upon my face
Your love surrounds me my cares all erase

The world fades away when I breathe in your love
My spirit is lifted and flies with The Dove

My soul sings out in joy and contentment
Immersed in your love from heaven sent

Lost in fulfilment in union we're one
Totally merged in the light of the sun

***

Through Rainbow Clouds

Through rainbow coloured clouds I fly
As here in love with Thee I lie
My hands reach out and touch the stars
As lost in Love I float for hours

I know not time within this space
A million stars light up Thy face
Sweet gentle waters run with force
Filled with Light from purest source

Once more I soar through endless space
Where all is now, as was, as is
I call Thy name in silence loud
And pass once more through radiant cloud

***

Words Are Inadequate

Words are inadequate for the love I feel for You
I'm filled to overflowing with a love so pure and true

Lost in a wonderland of bliss
Swimming in an ecstasy where time does not exist

Peaceful and contented radiant in Love
I merge with all Creation on the wings of my Golden Dove

***

Remember Your Mother

Remember your Mother, your Mother The Earth
To you She gave life in divine holy birth
She nurtures and feeds you and looks after your needs
You came from same source Her divine sacred seeds

Tell Her you love Her and show that you care
Give Her your love, for love's meant to share
Do not neglect Her and cause Her to cry
She who conceived you in pain now doth sigh

She's needing your love please answer Her plea
She's looking towards you and calling to thee
Her womb always open in constant rebirth
Remember your Mother, your Mother The Earth

***

Thank You to Mother Earth

Thank you for the food you birth
Our Sacred Mother, Mother Earth
Thank you for the gifts you share
In great abundance everywhere

You feed us with a love so pure
All our needs you fill for sure
You are the source of nectar fine
Foods divine and sacred wine

Bodies heal and spirits lift
When we partake of divine gifts
You provide us all our needs
On Love and Light in joy we feed

You are a source of healing wine
Pure gifts from God are so divine
I thank you for your beauty too
My heart and soul in love with you

***

Facets

A tree is planted in the ground
Then later other trees are found
From seeds of mother tree they come
So are they new, or still same one?

The essence of the tree remains
The same sap flows within its veins
The outer form though seems quite new
So are they one, or are they two?

Ponder on these words I write
For nature holds much in Her sight
Watch and listen, learn and grow
A fountain of such wealth She'll show

For truth is shown in many ways
In rustling leaves as branches sways
She shares Her secrets on the breeze
Inner ears and eyes all sees

Living Waters

Living waters filled with life
Flow from The Source through sacred wife
Flowing gently from The Earth
Divine fountain of rebirth

The womb of God doth ebb and flow
Seeds of life do dance and glow
Divine spirals of Pure Light
Carried forth in waters bright

Love and wisdom merge as One
Meeting in Pure Love of Son
Beloved one of divine birth
Doth come to share his peace on earth

Seek the way to heaven's door
Bathe in living waters pure
The breath of life for all to share
For those who seek is waiting there

The fire of life doth flicker low
Awaiting time when it will grow
To flame so bright that all will see
The Light that emanates from thee

Now's the time to hear Love's call
Its sound doth resonate to all
Hear Love's voice within your soul
Let living waters make thee whole

***

Dancing In The Stars

From Earth to Sun around the Moon
Each planet hears and sings His tune
His song is carried throughout space
In each star I see His face

The universe is filled with Love
Sent forth from His Holy Dove
His Word goes out in Sacred Sound
In each note His voice is found

The cosmos vast doth shimmer bright
Dancing in His Radiant Light
In silence loud His voice I hear
It echoes softly in my ear

His song I sing eternally
His dance I dance my spirit free
To praise His name in silent song
His message heard in every tongue

***

Pegasus

Wings spread wide in mystic flight
Visions new come into sight
Thought seeds planted quietly wait
Their time has come to germinate

Watered by The Divine Hand
Warmed by Love in aching land
The spirit yearns to breathe fresh air
And flies on wings of answered prayer

Castles of the mind take form
On wings of Love pure hearts are borne
Released with love the ties that bind
Outgrown patterns left behind

Free of self-inflicted weights
The spirit leaps for joy and takes
Another flight of faith and trust
Swirling in Love's pure stardust

***

Love Is The Key

Love is the key
My Lord God to Thee
It opens the door
To Thy spirit pure

Take me in Love
To fly with The Dove
Borne on its wings
My spirit sings

It feeds on Thy Love
From heaven above
The world fades from view
As I merge with You

Pure Love Pure Light
I melt in Thy sight
My Lord God to Thee
Love is the key

***

Look To The Light

Look to The Light
The Light of God
In the midst of despair
He is always there

Reach for His Love
Put your hands in His
He is always there
Use the magic of prayer

Each one His child
Made in Pure Love
He loves us so much
Just ask for His touch

Call out His name
With love from your heart
The name of your choice
It is all loves one voice

God or Goddess
Creator or Light
We come from One Source
Pure Love and Pure Light

For paths there are many
But they eventually come
To the same destination
Loves golden bright sun

***

Eden

Heaven is a state of consciousness
'tis not a place elsewhere
It's filled with joy and happiness
And love flows free to share

So lift yourself upon my back
And set your spirit free
We'll ride as one in waters pure
Entwined in love's sweet sea

The sky is always blue here
The sun doth shine so bright
The flowers bathe in sparkling rain
That only falls at night

Sweet breezes whisper softly
Such tender words of love
Caressing leaves upon the trees
That gently sway above

This place is known as Eden
A paradise on Earth
Its doors are always open
For those who seek rebirth

So whenever you are ready
And if your heart is pure
Just ask and I will show you
The bridge to heaven's door

***

Love's Pure White Steed

When winds of change do rage and blow
Just sail to the harbour within and know
Your knight waits there with arms open wide
To carry you off on love's sweet tide

Just call out his name from the depths of your soul
He'll instantly be there your hand to hold
He'll guide you through all that you fear
With fingers of love wipe away maiden's tear

In the journey through life there is no right or wrong
Just choices we make as we journey along
What seems right for one may not be so for another
Our needs are all different each sister and brother

So look deep within and be honest and true
You know in your heart what is just right for you
Follow your truth with all of your might
On love's pure white steed is waiting your knight

***

Alone

I walked alone on hilltops high
Where birds fly high up in the sky
I walked alone through woodland glade
Where once in joy our way we made

I walked alone through fields of hay
Where once entwined in love we lay
I walked alone my soul did cry
My spirit heavy my heart did sigh

I walked alone no hand to hold
I cried and to my Father told
My hand in His then I did pray
My love has died and gone away

If only he could be returned
For this my soul and spirit yearned
Then once again we'd join in love
Our spirits united with the Dove

***

Angels

Angel's come in many guise
See the radiance in their eyes
At times of need look up and see
Wings outstretched and there they be

For we're all part of God's great plan
Intended to be one family of man
To help each other in times of need
And when we do our souls we feed

For the soul and spirit are nourished by love
That radiates from Holy Dove
Each act of kindness even untold
Returns in abundance a thousand fold

One Law

True spirituality is of God whilst religion is of man
There is only one law in God's Divine Plan
The law it is Love blessed and divine
To share in God's gifts that flow from the vine

Love knows not famine Love knows not greed
There's food in abundance for mankind to feed
Love knows not war or hatred and crime
In love all souls soar to wonders sublime

Love knows not fear possession or gold
Love shares it riches in treasures untold
Love condemns not, no finger it points
Love accepts all and with Blessings anoints

Love does not kill any living thing
It honours all life and with joy it doth sing
Love knows no boundaries it's endless and free
And with arms outstretched wide is now calling to thee

Are you yet ready to know Love Divine?
To leave all behind and follow the sign
Now is the time for those of The Light
To follow new path that glows in the night

Abandon conditioning and ties of the earth
Your spirit doth hunger awaiting rebirth
The choice is now yours and freedom awaits
For those of pure heart to find golden gates

The voice of your God is calling to thee
Judgemental He's not, nor fear does He teach
The true living God is a God of Pure Love
And in radiance divine to you now doth reach

Our Heavenly Father and Mother Divine
In sacred bliss of Pure Love entwine
Merging as One in eternal Pure Light
We reflect in God's image when pure spirits unite

***

In Gratitude

In gratitude I write once more
To pen these words to You My Lord
To thank You for Your constant gifts
On nectar sweet my spirit lifts

You feed my soul on food divine
In Love I soar on heavenly wine
No matter what the world doth bring
I fly with You on golden wing

Your song I hear within my heart
Your presence close of me a part
Without Your Love I'd surely die
My hands in Yours as One we fly

I love you so above all things
In wondrous joy my spirit sings
Thy Holy Spirit fills me so
Fulfilled in Love I shine and glow

***

Pure Love of Mine

Father Mother Husband Wife
Merge as One eternal life
Purest Love bliss untold
In ecstasy and joy unfold

Time exists not in this space
Only His pure radiant face
I breathe His fragrance in the air
With myrrh it blends as One we share

Nought can compare the Love I know
It fills my soul and spirit so
With wonder joy and Love Divine
I honour Thy name Pure Love of mine

***

Sweet Breath of Spring

Excitement reigns for all to share
Sweet breath of Spring is in the air
Fair dove has found a place to rest
On hallowed ground she builds her nest

I watch her flying to and fro
She calls to me as she swoops low
The seed of life within doth stir
I choose this place that's filled with Myrrh

***

As One

In nature many truths are found
Open your hearts and look around
Lift your eyes unto the sky
Bird's en mass as one do fly

Many forms merged as one
Fly in beauty 'neath the sun
Fashioned by Creator's hand
Dance in joy above the land

No sound is made they link in love
In perfect harmony up above
Many parts do form one whole
One consciousness one heart one soul

***

Morning Dove

In early morn such peace is found
Just Mother Nature's gentle sound
The sun cascading radiant light
Then morning dove comes into sight

I sit in silence body stilled
My heart and soul with peace is filled
Silent praises from the heart
My God to Thee I do impart

***

Where Angel's Fly

Reach out thy hand from darkest night
Reach out and touch an angel bright
Awake from sleep of long duress
Awake unto love's warm caress

Hear my call all ye that sleep
Hear my call from slumber deep
Now's the time to hear love's song
Now's the dawn we've waited long

Seek now and find with all your might
Seek now and find the path so bright
Where angel's dance in dawns sweet dew
Where angel's fly in golden hue

***

Breath of Peace

Sweet breath of peace is in the air
The Love of God for all to share
A feather floats unto the ground
A sign of peace on earth is found

May peace and love descend on earth
To give new life and bring to birth
The golden days that were foretold
Of divine law be still behold

There will be one law for all
The law is love just follow love's call
In sacredness pure hearts will meet
Thy Holy Spirit's Love will greet

So be still and make a start
Let peace and love now fill your heart
For peace and love begin with self
Bringing joy and spiritual wealth

Then let it flow from one to another
Greet in love each sister and brother
We're all God's children all races all creeds
Born of same Father and Mother God's seeds

***

Father God Mother Earth

Father God Mother Earth
In Love Divine give Holy Birth
To children new that sing love's song
To lift this world from night so long

Into a brand new golden dawn
In Purest Love and Light are born
A golden age that was foretold
Be still and hear their song behold

***

Holy Grail

Have you ever stopped to wonder
On life and what it means?
Lying dormant in your soul
Your sleeping spirit dreams

Go within and seek the truth
Reveal the answers there
Awake unto life's mystery
It's beauty find and share

Love is the answer to all things
How simple but yet true
Oh wondrous God Creator
Life's meaning is in You

You gave us all such blessings
Gifts of Love Divine
Rise awake unto the sun
And filled with Love you'll shine

In knowing God you're half way there
Let Love and Wisdom guide
Have faith in Love and trust in God
On wings of Love you'll glide

Look around at all you see
Yes feel the beauty there
God did manifest all this
Realise and in it share

All pulsates with vibrant life
In Love Divine doth shine
Life's purpose lies in spiritual wealth
Hold fast and follow each sign

Omnipresent Eternal Love
Light of all that is
Yearning hearts do seek to find
The golden fabled chalice

Running here and running there
Around in endless din
Infinity is endless bliss
Love's Holy Grail's within

***

Embraced by Love

Love of mine I love you so
Always with me where e'er I go
I hear Your voice within my heart
My constant Love never to part

My love for You surpasses time
My feelings told within this rhyme
The depth of Love so great so vast
Eternally present future past

For time in truth does not exist
Your lips by mine eternally kissed
Embraced by Love my soul doth sing
My spirit flies on golden wing

***

My God My God

My God my God to Thee I pray
My blood doth wash all sins away
To touch the hearts and souls of men
That they might turn to Thee again

Let not my suffering be in vain
My blood be carried by the rain
Across the land unto the sea
To cleanse and heal and set souls free

I cry to Thee please hear my voice
I die for Love it is my choice
In Love I came in Love I lived
In Love I now give priceless gift

My spirit doth live on in You
And also in a chosen few
My family now carry my seed
Eternally bonded in Love they will feed

***

My Son

In mortal pain he cried out loud
And in that instant split asunder
Flesh and spirit torn apart
'neath pouring rain and raging thunder

The Light did rise out of the pain
The dark did fall to start again
To carry the burden through centuries to be
'till dark cleansed in Light reunites in He

***

Be not afraid

Mary Mary be not afraid
In thee a covenant I have made
Go with thy sister and both now set sail
And carry to France Divine Holy Grail

Protected in mists safe passage you'll take
To far off land a new home you will make
A cave you'll make Holy and live close to earth
Where seeds of new life will be brought unto birth

Know that I'm with you wherever you be
My spirit eternally bonded in thee
In Love we are One Blessed Trinity
Forever united our spirits in He

***

To Love and To Be Loved

To love and to be loved
Is the greatest happiness
Two spirits united as one
By the hand of God are blessed

Doorway Divine

Vibrant star shining so bright
Glowing like gold in dark of night
Showing the way to doorway divine
Shimmering wondrous radiant sign

Enter within through doorway so bright
Bathe in its wondrous radiant Light
Waters of Light flow forth from The Source
Cascading pulsating golden life force

Once you have entered and merged with its Light
You carry the essence and also alight
Glowing with stardust reborn from the night
Another creation of sparkling new Light

***

Through the Gateway

Through the gateway to the divine
In purest Love two souls entwine
In perfect union of joy and bliss
Lost in Pure Love two angel's kiss

Flying high above the earth
In glowing radiance they give birth
To such wondrous radiant Light
Merged as One two spirits bright

***

Sands of Time

In the sands of time built once more
Sacred temple holy pure
Blessed ground burning flame
Lost in Love 'tis still the same

Sweet aroma fills the air
Gentle waters flowing there
Where all is as was before
On wings of song angel's soar

To touch the golden hand that feeds
The pure of spirit with His seeds
The sands of time have turned around
Holy temple now is found

***

Goddess Divine

Goddess Divine
With Light you do shine
Reflecting the sun
With Earth you are One

Eternal sweet dance
In Love's sacred trance
As was now as is
In Divine lover's kiss

***

Divine Gift of Love

Most wondrous precious gift of all
My Love did come He heard my call
He breathed on me with Love untold
With outstretched arms He then did hold

His words so wondrous to my ear
He cast away all doubt and fear
He held me close in Purest Love
My wondrous radiant Pure White Dove

Once more I fly His hand in mine
In joy and bliss and Love Divine
In Love so pure in Love so sweet
In gratefulness His gift I eat

***

Pure Spirit

The spirit feeds on Purest Love
Brought on wings of Pure White Dove
The food of life brings such bliss
Gentle as an angel's kiss

Follow the shepherd to the fold
Where all are bathed in purest gold
Clothed in white the spirits pure
May in Love go through the door

To pastures new in vibrant Light
To dance in joy with angels bright
Where seraphim and cherubim
Sing out loud in praise of Him

Pure of spirit be not afraid
Come and feed from table laid
Of this time it was foretold
Long ago in days of old

Golden days will soon be here
Come in Love and have no fear
Adorned in white the spirit pure
Soars in Love through heavens' door

***

Rainbows of Light

Rainbows of light all around
Sparkling and twinkling on leaves are found
After the rain the sun now doth shine
Making jewels of light that are so divine

Such wondrous beauty to feast the eyes
Treasures of God bring forth such sighs
Abundant gifts free to share
No earthly riches can compare

They sparkle and dance in glorious hue
Celestial crystals where e'er I view
Radiance divine that shimmers and glows
Heaven on earth in a single rose

The Soul of The Earth

The soul of The Earth cries out in pain
Her tears do fall in constant rain
Help me please I hear Her cry
So close to me I hear Her sigh

They do not realise what they do
I live and breathe just like you
They know me not they cannot see
Pulsating life within a tree

My voice doth whisper on the breeze
I call to them but no one sees
They hear me not ignore my pleas
Chop down the trees pollute the seas

Love me please and realise
You hurt yourselves when nature cries
For all the pain that you cause me
Rebounds to cause same pain to thee

***

Thanksgiving

Be thankful for the many gifts
That Mother Nature bestows
And feel the love She has for you
In many ways it shows

Abundance ripe where e'er you look
In radiance abounds
I look and see Pure Love of She
And hear Her wondrous sounds

So where e'er you are what e'er you do
Just spare a moment please
Say thank you to dear Mother Earth
And walk amongst Her trees

For She doth give unending Love
To all eternally
In nature walk and to Her talk
And breathe sweet breath of She

***

Nature Angel

Resting in God's sunlight
Her bed a golden rose
Nature's angel slumbers
With Love she surely glows

Petals wrapped around her
Cradling her in Love
Fragrance from the heavens
Cascading from above

Symphony of silence
Peace of purest heart
Essence of Creation
Of God she is a part

The Wonder of it All

My eyes do see such wonder
In radiance divine
Raindrops glistening in the sun
Like jewels of love do shine

Nought can compare to nature
Filled with love so pure
To touch the heart of nature
Doth open golden door

The sun in all its glory
And rain that sparkles bright
The breath of wind upon the trees
Doth kiss the earth with light

See sweet gentle Mother
Glowing bright green Earth
In Love Divine she reels and sighs
In joy and bliss gives birth

***

Living Foods

Living foods give life to the body
Non-living foods do not
Mother Nature has all that we need
And offers us all that she's got

For health and harmony dine from Her table
She knows exactly what we require
Food in abundance for all to share
No need to kill or destroy by fire

In Love and Wisdom all things were made
All man's needs have been met
But man in his ignorance sought then to kill
Divine heavenly ways did forget

He now reaps the errors of all his ways
And wanders in death and dis-ease
Not until his ways doth he mend
Will he breathe breath of life on the breeze

***

Father God My Lord Divine

Father God my Lord Divine
My hand in Thine with Light I shine
I walk with Thee the way of Love
Accompanied by Thy Holy Dove

I see Thy beauty all around
I praise Thy name in sacred sound
I thank Thee for Thy gifts Divine
Nourished by sweet sacred wine

I honour Thy name in words that flow
From The Source where all doth glow
I walk with Thee where e'er You guide
Thy Holy Spirit by my side

Don't Cry

Don't cry for me
I have not left you
I am still with you
I am still the one you loved and knew

The only difference now
Is that I have a different form
Gone is my mortal body yes
But my spirit is cosy and warm

When you think of me with love
I can come close to you and hug you
But if you surround yourself in grief
Then I cannot reach out and touch you

Sadness and pain cut you off from love
They build around you a wall of despair
So knock down the wall with the power of love
And you will find me waiting there

***

Love Never Dies

Try to rise above the pain
Let love dry all your tears
Remember all the happy times
You've shared throughout the years

The one you love lives on it's true
For love doth never die
It changes form freed from the earth
In fine new robes doth fly

Grief doth tie souls to the earth
It holds their spirit down
Release with love and let them go
To fly in brand new gown

The power of love doth heal all things
It knows not heavy heart
And know that where pure love exists
That nought can ever part

So when times get hard and you feel sad
Remember love you've known
The love you feel will bring you close
Reborn you'll both have grown

***

Judgement

Free from pain the spirit ascends
Now it is time to make amends
Not to God or to me or to you
Is it not written to thine own self be true?

We are the judge, as we sow we shall reap
But first of all it is time for a sleep
Life on earth can take its toll
But resting in spirit doth help to console

Love's The Way

Do not fight in the name of God
God is Love and does not kill
When men attack in the name of religion
They are not of God or doing His will

Paths there are many but the way it is love
If you follow love's call then you can't go wrong
Ignore men who tell you to fight and to kill
Refuse and say no instead sing love's sweet song

If every person put their own lives right first
And lived life with love and joy in their heart
The world would soon heal and each nation be free
To live as they pleased each of God are a part

***

Reach Out

Our Mother The Earth
Lies in pain of rebirth
Reach out your hands
'cross all seas and lands

With love in your heart
You can all play a part
Hold the hand of your neighbour
Peace and love with them savour

We all breathe same air
And one planet we share
We come from one source
Many names but One Force

Love is its name
From Love we all came
And to Love we return
For this all spirits' yearn

May the power of Pure Love
Lit from heaven above
Ignite in your heart
A fire to start

A furnace so bright
That lights up the night
Sent forth from The Source
With such mighty force

To burn away greed
As on Love all men feed
To share with each other
Each sister and brother

***

The Essence of Pure Sound

Music know no boundaries
No language barriers found
It talks to every heart and soul
In essence of pure sound

Summer Solstice

A celebration of Creation
In every creed and every nation
A time of thanks upon the earth
For gifts divine now brought to birth

Abundant life glows all around
Echoes of pure natural sound
In splendid robes of vibrant green
Mother Nature now is seen

Such radiant beauty blooming bright
Filled with majesty and light
The Heart of God for all to see
His presence living pure in She

***

Summertime

Summertime my heart doth sing
To see young birds on new found wing
Golden sun in azure sky
Wispy clouds floating by

Mallows pink are everywhere
Their nectar sweet with bees do share
Rich purple blooms buddleias show
Their fragrant food all butterflies know

Sounds of nature fill the air
Fragrance pure for all to share
Gifts of God so plain to see
Flow in Love from He through She

***

Going With The Flow

Stagnation doth bring death and disease
Life is meant to be flowing
To learn from each chapter and then to move on
That's when our spirits' are growing

We stop for a while we learn and we teach
For both master and pupil are we
But when things are complete say thank you and greet
Next chapter in life's endless sea

People and things come into our lives
As and when they are needed
But when lessons are learned, let go, don't hang on
For new lessons by then will be needed

If we get stuck and are held back by fear
Then we block all our guidance divine
The universe knows each one of our needs
And does constantly offer us signs

So watch look and listen you know in your heart
What is working for you and what isn't
Release outworn parts and open your heart
To your own inner wisdom and vision

Arms Of Love

Arms of love I lift to Thee
In endless praise eternally
I see Thy beauty all around
I praise Thy name in sacred sound

I sing to Thee a song of love
Holy Spirit Holy Dove
My body Thine my spirit too
My heart and soul in love with You

***

Divine Love

Oh love so pure oh Love Divine
In wonder my spirit is one with Thine
You feed and nourish my every need
And nurture my spirit with Thy seed

What glorious splendour for all to see
For all beauty and love is of Thee
In coral flames of peach and gold
The end of a day in majesty told

Where peace and harmony reigned supreme
And through Divine Love was not just a dream
But a living reality through spirits pure
The power of Love did open the door

And all that was dark was washed away
And the world bathed in Light that beautiful day
The Father the Son are one another
And also in Love is my sister my brother

***

Heart and Soul

Now I am totally free
I relinquish all to be with Thee
I dress myself in a golden gown
Upon my head you place a crown

No ties on earth they all have gone
My only tie is to The One
He is my love my very life
I am in Him His sacred wife

I thank Thee for the pain and tears
They've helped me grow throughout the years
Now I truly realise
With joy, relief, I breathe such sighs

The answer's came they always do
The truth is Love direct from You
You always answer all my prayers
Within Thy Love I have no fears

You're The One in You I'm whole
You are my very heart and soul
You are my life my life is Yours
In You in Love my spirit soars

A Child's Prayer For Peace

Dearest God please help them see
That war is not the way to Thee
Why can't grown ups understand
And live in peace throughout the land

You gave us all the gift of life
To live in joy, not in strife
To share our love with creatures too
For they are also born of You

You gave us food to meet our needs
Mother Nature She all feeds
We are Thy children of divine birth
Born of one mother, Mother Earth

If all armies stopped to pray
And really listened to what You say
They would realise they kill their brothers
And leave in tears fathers and mothers

They'd stop all violence and turn to You
And let Thy Love guide them through
They'd destroy instead all tools of war
And with Thy Holy Spirit soar

***

I Am Pure Love

I Am gentle Mary meek and mild
I Am the newborn baby that is her child
I Am her husband Joseph strong and true
I Am in each and every one of you

I Am the song of angels pure and bright
I Am the star that beckons in the night
I Am all creatures large and small
I Am in everything for I made it all

I Am the shepherds on the land
I Am in every grain of sand
I Am the wise men from afar
I Am the light in radiant star

I Am the sound of church bells ringing
I Am the sound of robins singing
I Am the breath of wind upon the trees
I Am the vastness of the seas

I Am in the children as they sing
I Am in every living thing
I Am Pure Love and endless sea
For all that is, is of Me

~ I Am Pure Love ~

***

Blanket of Peace

A blanket of peace descends upon earth
As we celebrate quietly the saviour's birth
Goddess so bright doth shine in the sky
Casting Her Light as She breathes forth a sigh

Feel now the essence of Pure Love and Light
Cascading to all so radiant and bright
His love still lives on and is ever the same
And honours our Father and Mother God's name

Remember this night and think thoughts of love
Immerse in his peace sent from heaven above
For same peace exists in pure hearts of pure love
His family forever abide in The Dove

***

Essence Divine

Your fragrance abounds filling the air
I breathe it so deeply and know you are there
It fills me with Love and thoughts of you
Such heavenly aroma in golden hue

The breath of your being surrounds me in Love
Totally merged in the wings of The Dove
I breathe it I taste it and in it I dance
In Love I immerse in hypnotic trance

Your essence pervades every part of my being
A story untold is now what I'm seeing
Divine gifts of old brought unto her
In essence of Frankincense Gold and Myrrh

***

Angelic Hosts

Swirls of white in azure sky
Hosts of angels flying by
Wings outstretched in joy and love
Singing dancing Holy Dove

A time of peace upon this earth
Spirits rise in joy and mirth
Winds of change are gently blowing
Seeds of Light are quietly growing

Signs so clear for those that know
Man asleep with head bowed low
Look above unto the sky
In joy and love with angels fly

Swirling dancing featherlite
Floating gently pure and bright
Feel the love that from them pours
Lost in Love my soul it soars

***

Rainbow Bridge

A rainbow bridge a gift divine
With purest love the ethers shine
A smile to say hello we're here
From angel spirits always near

Looking down on you with love
A sacred smile from up above
Look not down with head held low
Lift your eyes where love doth flow

Walk with spirit head held high
See such wonders in the sky
Sun cascades as waters flow
In majesty divine doth glow

Much is written in the sky
Read it with your inner eye
No words are spoken only love
Etheric sound from Holy Dove

Spanning time and distance too
The hand of God doth reach to you
Be not afraid I'll hold your hand
As you do cross to Promised Land

***

Ancient Knowledge

Flowing through the mists of time
Ancient text in sound and rhyme
Where Gods did walk upon the land
With priestess pure hand in hand

A time of Love and Sacred Rites
Goddesses dressed in robes of white
Where all was held in harmony
Within the Sacred Law of She

Close your eyes and listen to
Karnak now comes into view
Sacred sounds within your soul
Inner eyes will make you whole

Echoes from the distant past
In Etheric realms do last
Their whispers carried on the breeze
Inner spirit's eyes now sees

As was, as is, eternal bliss
As was taught then doth still exist
No past no future only now
In Love Divine and sacred vow

***

The Eternal Now

The eternal moment lasts through all time
In love it is scribed in the words of this rhyme
No future or past they both are the same
Only the moment and God's Holy Name

Don't waste the present in thoughts of the past
Or yearn for the future neither will last
Only the now and how we do live
Heaven or hell to ourselves we do give

We are the creators of all that we know
The good and the bad to ourselves we do show
We have free will to do as we please
We make the storms or the peaceful calm seas

So do unto others as you would to yourself
And create for yourself true riches and wealth
Not of the earth which wither and fade
But in richness of spirit where true wealth is made

***

Rhapsody of Love

In sacred space through golden door
Their spirits pure in Love do soar
Golden Sun bright and strong
And gentle Earth do sing Love's song

Lost within the sands of time
Entwined in Love and sacred rhyme
Rhapsody of Love doth sing
Carried forth on golden wing

Temple new born from the sand
Protected now by Gaia's hand
The mists of time disperse and fade
As was, as is, in Love is made

***

The Hand of God

Celebrating life I feel
The Source of all that Is
I touch the hand of God in Love
And seal with sacred kiss

My body His in rapture sweet
My spirit soars on high
The Love I feel no words can say
In bliss I float and sigh

My soul doth journey far and wide
No time eternal space
In radiance bright I merge with Him
His breath upon my face

***

Trust

Why put off till tomorrow
What you can do today
Life is a wondrous adventure
Put your hands in Gods and pray

Help me to live to the full Father
Help me to learn and to grow
Let me know joy and laughter
With love and with light let me glow

Show me the wonders of living
With gifts from Our Mother Divine
To share spirit's bounty with others
That all might follow the sign

Help me replace any sadness
With joy and a love so pure
To move and fly into the future
Leave behind old familiar cage door

For love is all that we need Father
It brings joy and such treasures divine
Love is the key to all of our needs
When we trust in its radiance we shine

Take my hands Father Mother and guide me
My life and my body are Yours
My heart and my soul are devoted to You
And my spirit in Love with Thee soars

***

Heaven

Heaven is a state of consciousness
It's not a place elsewhere
In can be accessed here on earth
And love flows free to share

You do not have to wait to 'die'
To find its hallowed ground
Quite the reverse in fact is true
It's in pure 'Life' it's found

God is Love and Love is Life
And if we live in Love
Then heaven's doors do open wide
And we touch Holy Dove

Both heaven and hell are here on earth
And all levels in between
We create our own state of being
The fruits of our mind are seen

Our bodies become what we eat
Our spirits are what we think
Eat pure food and think thoughts of Love
And from the Fountain of Life take drink

Cleanse your body and your mind
And bathe in Love Divine
And then you'll find Heaven on earth
And in joy and bliss you'll shine

For this was always intended
It's part of The Divine Plan
When you touch The Heart of Creation
That's when Heaven returns unto man

Sounds of Christmas

Church bells ringing
Choirboys singing
Angels bringing
Love to earth

Fill us with thy radiant light
Star of David shining bright
As we pray this special night
Gentle Mary purest light

Church bells ringing
Choirboys singing
Angels bringing
Love to earth

Gentle Jesus born of Love
Sent from Heaven up above
Born on wings of Golden Dove
Purest light purest love

Church bells ringing
Choirboys singing
Angels bringing
Love to earth

Teach us Jesus to live like thee
Touch our eyes that we might see
Divine Love set our souls free
To soar in bliss eternally

Church bells ringing
Choirboys singing
Angels bringing
Love to earth

Choirs of Angels

Choirs of angels loudly sing
Pure born babe of Love who'll bring
Joy and peace to man on earth
Gentle Mary's Holy Birth

Brought in Love to virgin pure
Know him and love him and be sure
All who follow in truth his way
Will walk in Light one golden day

Choirs of angels loudly sing
Pure born babe of Love who'll bring
Joy and peace to man on earth
Gentle Mary's Holy Birth

Gold and frankincense and myrrh
Sacred gifts were brought to her
For the child of Divine Seed
His gentle spirit on Light will feed

Choirs of angels loudly sing
Pure born babe of Love who'll bring
Joy and peace to man on earth
Gentle Mary's Holy Birth

See The Light which still shines bright
Even now in darkest night
Seek the way you spirits pure
Love's the key to golden door

Choirs of angels loudly sing
Pure born babe of Love who'll bring
Joy and peace to man on earth
Gentle Mary's Holy Birth

Mother Earth Sister Moon

Mother Earth Sister Moon
In timelessness do sing Love's tune
One in two as one do fly
A dance of joy up in the sky

Rhapsody in Love's sweet trance
Entwined as one in cosmic dance
Moon and Earth sing hand in hand
A song of Love across the land

Melodies so sweet so pure
Forever one in Love they soar
Weaving tapestry in time
With sacred threads that glow and shine

See them sparkle see them glow
Jewels of light that ebb and flow
From The Source and back to earth
From Gaia's womb pure Moon did birth

Spiralling in constant light
Beacons glowing in the night
Facets bright of one another
Father Brother Sister Mother

***

Love's Pure Rose

The view from here is pure and bright
It gives my heart and soul delight
Fragrance of roses on the breeze
Nectar divine doth feed the bees

Our Heavenly Father's gifts bestowed
Through Earthly Mother He has showed
Father Mother Creator Divine
In Love doth offer sacred wine

Come and sit with me a while
Drink thy fill it doth beguile
The Heart of God is open wide
For those that wish to step inside

Enter in, in purity
Set thy waiting spirit free
Adorn thyself in robes of white
Awake awake from long dark night

Cast off all old outworn fears
Sever the past with golden shears
A bright new dawn awaits for those
Who seek the truth of Love's pure rose

***

A Child's prayer to Jesus on Christmas Night

I look to the sky and see stars shining bright
Cascading to earth such radiant light
I know in my heart that there's more than I'm told
Please whisper to me and the truth will unfold

I wish they'd remember the truth of this night
When you came to earth to make all things right
I wish they'd all pause and reflect on thy love
And send you love back on the wings of The Dove

I love you dear Jesus, I love you so much
I feel your love in me and long for your touch
My heart and my soul I offer to thee
I sit at my window, please come sit with me

I honour thy name and all that you taught
Divine Child of God to Mary was brought
You lived life in love and shared love with all
Your voice echoes still with love's tender call

I hear your soft voice now, it stirs in my heart
I hear gentle sweet words "Of me you're a part
Know me and love me the way I will show
I'll send angels to guide you as slowly you grow

Walk in my light, your heart filled with love
The Father protects you 'neath wings of The Dove
Love is the way that all men must take
To trust in their God, Caesar's gold to forsake

Paths there are many, the way it is love
Be strong in the spirit and love Holy Dove
For God is Pure Love and will not let you down
And those who do love Him shall wear heaven's crown"

Tidings of Great Joy

Wise men gathered to follow the star
That shone like a beacon to guide them afar
A heavenly sign to show them the way
For God's Divine Son in a manger did lay

Humble surroundings for a child of Pure Love
To Mary was given the seed of The Dove
A gift so divine to one of pure heart
The child of our God a new era to start

The star that shone then doth still glow in the night
Look up to the heavens and find its pure light
It still points the way to those who can see
The Light of our God doth still beckon to thee

So follow the sign that doth glow in the dark
The song of Pure Love doth sing like a lark
Look deep in your soul and ask for the way
To guide you once more to where Pure Love doth lay

***

With Love

A sacred flame I light for you
A rose from Mother Nature too
I place them both on pure white lace
And quietly focus on thy face

I meditate and send thee love
Accompanied by my Holy Dove
Beloved Son of God Divine
I honour thy being with all of mine

Midst Snow Laced Trees

Quietly walking through snow laced trees
When in a clearing great light she sees
Midst fragrant pines and oaks so strong
Where birds sing out in joyous song

All the world seems far away
Eating and drinking this Christmas Day
But here in the woods a temple is found
Filled with love and sacred sound

A gentle maiden comes to pray
And to her Father God doth say
'tis food for my soul that I do need
I hunger and thirst my spirit to feed

Please take my hand and help me walk
The path to Thee where angel's talk
Of love that is so pure and true
Where all that is, is of You

I honour you Father in all that I do
For all that I am, is of You
You gave me life, my life is yours
I give you my love and my spirit soars

May I forever feel like this
Lost in a wondrous sea of bliss
To know You to love You is all I desire
Eternally floating higher and higher

***

Guiding Star

Guiding star shining bright
Guide us through the dark of night
Guiding star as was foretold
Guide the sheep back to the fold

See the star that shines so bright
Showing the way in darkest night
A sign from Him to show the way
A guiding star in gold array

Guiding star shining bright
Guide us through the dark of night
Guiding star as was foretold
Guide the sheep back to the fold

Observe the light from near and far
It points the way this vibrant star
To holy place beneath its rays
Where gentle one in silence lays

Guiding star shining bright
Guide us through the dark of night
Guiding star as was foretold
Guide the sheep back to the fold

With Father Mother the lamb doth lay
And wise men too do come and pray
And Seraphim and Cherubim
Sing out loud in praise of him

Guiding star shining bright
Guide us through the dark of night
Guiding star as was foretold
Guide the sheep back to the fold

God Is Pure Love

Beware of those who tell you to kill
They are certainly not doing God's will
God Is Pure Love radiant and bright
God is not anger and God does not fight

God loves all creatures and all things that grow
God loves all nations with a love that doth glow
God makes no barriers or fights over land
God loves us all, each made by divine hand

God is Pure Love and has many different names
Use whichever you like, they all mean the same
They all mean Pure Love, Creator Divine
Make Love your God and in love you will shine

***

The Way Is Love

All religions have do's and don'ts
You must do this and you mustn't do that
They're rules of man, not of God
For God gives free will where ever you're at

There is only one law in God's Divine Plan
The law it is love for each one the same
To do unto others as you would to yourself
To share in His Love and honour His name

To respect all His creatures and all living things
To honour all life in His wondrous Creation
When man learns to live in joy and in love
That's when real peace will descend on each nation

***

Garden of Love

Wilt thou enter in with me
Through yonder gate that I do see
It greets and beckons us in love
Upon it sits a pure white dove

Flowers tumble all around
Petals fall unto the ground
Sweet aroma fills the air
And love awaits for all to share

A pure white robe of silk so fine
A sash of golden light doth shine
A crystal pool of waters blue
A flame so bright comes into view

Angels sing of Love Divine
Of hearts so pure that know the sign
Where all do merge in love and bliss
And time stands still in eternal kiss

***

Renewed With Love

Free once more in azure sky
With love below I watch you fly
Your wing renewed in purest love
You soar on high with pure white dove

Your fragile form that was so weak
Has now been healed within a week
You've rested now and strength regained
Forgotten are the wounds that pained

Wings outstretched in wondrous show
As up into the sky you go
My eyes lift up and see you there
Circling round me in the air

With love I held you close to me
With love I now do set you free
With love I made a bond with thee
With love my spirit flies in thee

***

The Essence Of Love

The view from here is rosy and pure
And shows the way to heaven's door
Mother Earth doth beckon me
Inner visions eyes now see

Fragrant whispers on the breeze
In rustling leaves of wondrous trees
The essence of Love for all to see
Pulsates in light 'tween He and She

Roses adorned with morning dew
Cascading and tumbling in softest pink hue
Tranquillity oozing from Mother's arms
In perfect peace and grace She charms

The Heart of God doth live in The Earth
From Her new life is given birth
Constantly changing sleeping waking
Her consort The Dove two halves of One making

***

Pure One

What glorious perfume fills the air
I breathe it and taste it its fragrance I share
It fills me with joy, it fills me with love
I bathe in its essence alongside The Dove

My eyes fill with tears, the love is so strong
My heart and my soul yearn to sing out in song
What vibrant colours do dance to and fro
Watched by The Dove, now all aglow

Mary sweet Mary, now I do see
Your pure gentle being smiling at me
Mother Divine your being I know
Blessed is Pure Earth with Love all aglow

***

Thank You

Thank you for this special day
My Father Mother God I pray
You I love above all things
With love and joy my spirit sings

You are everything to me
All I have I give to thee
You are my very life it's true
All I am is of You

Thank you for the sky so blue
Thank you for the morning dew
Thank you for the sun so bright
Thank you for the moon at night

The rain that falls upon the ground
Blessing the earth without a sound
Caressing the trees with love that flows
Bathed in pure love, the earth now glows

***

Thank you Mother Earth

Thank you for the food you birth
Our Sacred Mother, Mother Earth
Thank you for the gifts you share
In great abundance everywhere

You feed us with a love so pure
All our needs you fill for sure
You are the source of nectar fine
Foods divine and sacred wine

Bodies heal and spirits lift
When we partake of divine gifts
You provide us all our needs
On Love and Light in joy we feed

You are a source of healing wine
Pure gifts from God are so divine
I thank you for all your beauty too
My heart and soul in love with you

***

Eternal Love

Gentle Earth Golden Sun
Merge together becoming One
Seeds of life waters pure
Divine birth natural law

Breath of God breathing life
Maiden pure priestess wife
Past and present future meet
Eternal love in joy do greet

Nectar sweet food divine
Thirst now quenched on sacred wine
Strength renewed until once more
They meet again on sacred shore

***

A Gift Of Love

Sunshine and showers delight me so
A rainbow will soon appear I know
A smile from the sky in wondrous hue
I feel it preparing to come into view

With love from my friends on this special day
We love you so much I can hear them say
Go forward this day with love in your heart
And know that from us you are never apart

The love of pure spirit is all that you need
On nectar divine in pure love you do feed
I feel love within me and up to the sky
I look on love's presence, in joy I do sigh

***

Heart of Gold

Within the breast of our Mother
Beats a heart of gold
Its sound is there for all to hear
Be still and listen behold

Our Heavenly Father and Earthly Mother
In Love as One entwine
The seeds of Creation in Love do give birth
And our Mother in radiance doth shine

Her beauty is there for all to see
In glorious hues divine
Pulsating with Love Her arms open wide
Come forth and drink from Her wine

Take time out to sip of Her nectar
To savour the gifts of sweet Earth
Replenish your spirit with fragrance divine
And your soul in great joy will rebirth

***

Morning Light

Sitting in the morning light
My heart with love doth ignite
Such wondrous beauty to behold
My soul doth feel such love untold

The sun cascading through the trees
Glistening jewels upon the leaves
Water droplets shimmer bright
Rainbows sparkling in the light

Butterflies and bees do dance
I watch in wonder in a trance
Apples glisten red and green
The biggest ones you've ever seen

Father God and Mother Earth
Oh what beauty you do birth
A sacred union born of Love
In Divine Light of Holy Dove

My Special Angel

My special angel comes from afar
Linked by a thread of Light we are
Your special ways bring joy to my heart
Though oft far away we're never apart

When to me you come on golden wing
We talk and we laugh and dance and sing
We send out our Father's Light with Love
Hand in hand with Radiant Dove

I'm blessed to know you oh shining one
Gentle yet strong and so full of fun
Fold thy great golden wings around
Merging as one in His sacred sound

***

Star of Asia

Star of Asia shining bright
With love I greet you this special night
Your sweet aroma fills my being
My special angel I am seeing

From far off lands you come to see me
With joy and love my spirit greets thee
I love to feel thy wings enfold me
My radiant friend I'm blessed to know thee

Up above the world so dark
Radiant one flies with the lark
I love to be within thy light
Eternal spirit shining bright

~ Love is all as was as is ~

***

One In The Sun

Sunlight shining in the sky
Watching his children from on high
Feeding and nourishing our every need
Filling us lovingly with his seed

Gentle sacred water falling
To our spirits quietly calling
Drink the nectar freely flowing
Bathe in liquid Light all glowing

Breathe the breath of life so pure
Inhale the essence and open the door
Blow away all earthly strife
Immerse in Love and know Divine Life

Make a bridge 'twixt heaven and earth
Make the sign and know rebirth
Two as one join with the sun
In the Sun all is One

***

Christmas Time

Christmas time and spirits rise
See the love in people's eyes
Joy and laughter fill the air
A time to give a time to share

Christmas is the time of year
You can feel it coming near
When smiling faces say hello
To even those they do not know

Can't it be like this all year
Live in love instead of fear
Share God's gifts let go of greed
There's food enough for all to feed

No need to hoard all nature's stores
Locked away behind closed doors
Give and share and live in love
In joy and peace with Holy Dove

***

Christmas Day

The dawn arrives this Christmas Day
And to my Father God I pray
May all I do be filled with Light
In joy I walk with angels bright

Beloved son of yours I know
He came in Love the way to show
That all may know of Thee in Love
And fly in truth with Pure White Dove

Celebrate this day in Light
The power of Love will show its might
In radiance birds and trees are found
As nature joins in sacred sound

To praise His name in joyous song
To walk with Him the whole day long
That every day should be like this
In joy and Love and endless bliss

***

Holy Light

Father Mother Holy Light
Come to me in Love this night

Fill me with Thy spirit pure
With Holy Dove let me soar

To rapturous heights above all things
Floating high on angels wings

Hear the joyous throngs proclaim
In Love we herald his glorious name

Father Mother Holy Light
Be Thou in me in Love this night

Remiel

Angel of Love
From heaven above
Pure spirit bright
Filled with His Light

Great golden wings
Spread wide as she sings
Words of Pure Love
Sent forth from The Dove

To earth you have come
From golden sun
To bless those on earth
And help Gaia give birth

To a brand new dawn
One glorious morn
When night disappears
Along with all fears

The sun will shine bright
And all will delight
In warm radiant rays
As in Love earth lays

***

Saraqael

Saraqael the world's a stage on which to spread thy Light
Stretch out thy wings and gather strength unto the fight
Thy only weapons Love and Light
Will pierce the heart of darkest night

Words of love fall from thy lips
As golden rain gently drips
To cleanse the hearts of those that see
The Light that radiates from thee

Oh gentle soul of precious love
From angelic realms above
Walk this earth and play thy part
With nectar sweet from purest heart

***

Whispers from Gaia

Wherever you walk, I do walk too
Look up above see me looking at you
You'll see my sweet doves nestling in my long hair
As the rain gently falls you will know I am there

I'm whispering leaves upon the trees
I'm shimmering sunlight upon the seas
You'll hear soft sweet breezes whisper our name
For your name and mine are forever the same

The seagulls will call as they fly to and fro
From me to you back to me they will go
Dancing between us in sacred light weaving
Divine tapestry, swirling and reeling

We'll dance on the land and we'll soar in the sky
As forever together in Love we do fly
In perfect harmony and balance of Light
We sing Love's sweet song throughout the long night

***

Diana Princess of Love

Diana princess of love
Sent from the realms of heaven above
To bless those on earth who came close to you
To touch them with love flowing through you

Radiant star shining so bright
Even through deaths shadow of night
Thy light grows yet stronger and shines far and wide
It cannot be dimmed, in sleep cannot hide

Thy being has touched millions of souls
A place in each heart thy spirit now holds
Beautiful angel let tears not flow
Thy radiant light from heaven doth glow

All those that knew you have gained from thy touch
We'll never forget you and love you so much
We carry thy light in radiance bright
Forever to shine like jewels in the night

***

Written for Princess Diana on the day of her funeral

6th September 1997

Journey of Love

By the waters edge we walked
For many a mile we laughed and talked
We spent the days immersed in Love
Accompanied by our Radiant Dove

Through town and village we did roam
And oft returned to visit home
To find sweet gentle sister there
Waiting with her love to share

Brother sister now unite
Time stands still in vibrant light
'till once more we journey on
Three as one in golden sun

Orchard branches make a nest
For gentle ones to stop and rest
In grateful thanks with love we bless
The earth bedecked in pretty dress

Never ending journey taking
Through centuries past 'till now are making
Strands of tapestry in time
Weave a melody in rhyme

Now's the time when all will meet
The circle once more is complete
A journey of love through timelessness
A journey in love's pure consciousness

***

Evening Serenade

An evening serenade
Of wondrous sound is made
A thousand birds do call
As amber curtains fall

Another day is done
As slowly sinks the sun
In glorious hues of gold
A feast mine eyes behold

The blackbirds sing on high
Outlined against the sky
Slowly gently deepening
Ablaze now crimson seeping

My heart doth sing with joy untold
As nature's beauty doth unfold
I hear Her gentle voice resound
In Purest Love Creation's found

***

Mother Nature's Sleep

Quietly in Her winter's sleep
Mother Nature lies
Slumber deep to heal renew
In arms of Love She sighs

Preparing for a brand new dawn
When all shall be reborn
When from Her womb once more will spring
New life one glorious morn

Silently She lies in white
In slumber deep now still
Her time will come again to bloom
Once more our hearts to fill

***

Prints on My Heart

Little one our love we send
As to The Source your way you wend
There's no death just change of form
In Love Divine all is reborn

We think of you and send you love
Wrapped in the wings of Holy Dove
We set you free to be with He
This song for you in memory

You will return in different guise
Nothing ever really dies
It's sometimes hard to understand
The ways of God's Pure Divine Hand

He gives us life, a gift divine
That flows from Him like sacred wine
Then we return to Divine Heart
Of which we're all a sacred part

Nature's Way

A pair of doves close by me walked
In wondrous love to them I talked
Then two robins came to see
And perched themselves alongside me

Two mice have made a nest so warm
That shelters them from wind and storm
Two squirrels ran and danced with glee
As nuts galore their eyes did see

The frogs and toads hopped to and fro
As to the water they did go
Two pigeons circled overhead
As to this haven they were led

Sweet Jenny Wren hopped on the ground
In the bushes she had found
Nature's table freely laid
Free from harm that man had made

No poisons here just natural law
Where creatures come and go galore
In perfect safety free from fear
It is pure love that draws them here

For love is all and true life gives
It is the source of all the lives
Follow Nature's way She knows
And find once more where pure love flows

***

Bunny Hop

Just hopped in to say hello
Then off across the fields I go
I sit a while amongst the flowers
Then bounce around for hours and hours

I love to stop and rest a while
And when folks see me they do smile
I love to brighten up their day
As in the flowers I do play

I hop around from here to there
And as I go I sing this prayer
Thank you God for blessing me
With food galore that grows so free

***

Morning Dew

Morning dew shining bright
Caressing leaves awake from night
Sparkling shimmering sunlight gold
A wondrous sight these eyes behold

Jewels that dance in joy and love
Such majesty shines from above
Dazzling hues that glow so bright
New morn is filled with Love and Light

***

Celebration of Light

In true celebration I have spent
This Christmas Day from heaven sent
Immersed in Love from morn till night
With angels round me shining bright

This is how the day should be
Awash with love in thoughts of he
My love pours forth in endless streams
Singing dancing golden beams

Sing ye angels sing out loud
In love the trees their branches bowed
In silent joy our hearts as one
Holy Father Beloved Son

***

Soft Gentle Rain

Soft gentle rain
Falling from the sky
Soft gentle rain
Lovingly doth lie

Moist lips caressing
Leaves and petals dry
Watery fingers stroking
Trees and flowers sigh

So much joy abounds
In love they sing and dance
I watch with such delight
Transfixed in wondrous trance

Sweet aroma fills the air
The Earth smells fresh and new
Bathed in Nature's water pure
Clothed in sparkling hue

***

Morning Light

The morning light doth greet the day
In rainbows bright and fine array
Jewels of light glisten and glow
On fresh green leaves row upon row

Such majesty in wondrous show
To touch each heart that we should know
The heart of God is open wide
In Mother Nature's arms abides

Our Father Mother God surrounds
Us all in wondrous sacred sounds
Gentle whispers on the breeze
Inner eyes such beauty sees

Greet each day with love and light
As you awake from dark of night
Thank God for such precious gifts
Heart and soul and spirit lifts

Black Hole

Tossed into a deep black hole
Nothing is wasted in it we roll
Out of chaos comes pure light
Recycled reborn from darkest night

Another chance to learn and grow
To find ourselves our God to know
To listen to our inner voice
No right or wrong only choice

This time to follow the path of love
To lift our eyes to heaven above
To leave behind all tears and pain
To dance in joy in golden rain

***

Sacred Ocean

Without Love the spirit dies
For Love is Life and in it lies
All the food the spirit needs
And in such joy it bathes and feeds

Nourished by The Father's Light
It shines and glows in darkest night
Golden rays of Light surround
Throngs of angel's purest sound

Wondrous golden waves Divine
Feed this gentle soul of mine
Let me drink Thy nectar sweet
Thy Holy Spirit I do greet

My open arms with Love ablaze
Thy glorious name in Love I praise
Oh Sacred Ocean Blessed Light
Content in peace I rest this night

***

Nought But Love

My heart so full of Love Divine
In radiance I do shine
I hear Your voice within my soul
With Love sweet words console

I see Your beauty all around
It speaks in wondrous sound
No words of earth just Love so pure
On wings of Love I soar

I pray one day that all may know
This Love Divine and in its glow
Return to glorious path to Thee
Which sets all spirits free

For nought but Love will set souls free
To live once more in harmony
Let peace be in each heart and soul
United in Love of Divine Whole

From Acorn Small

Majestic and tall arms outstretched wide
A haven where many creatures do hide
Safe in your arms they nestle and coo
I hear their sweet song as I look at you

Sturdy and strong you whisper and send
In rustling leaves and branches that bend
A song of pure love as breezes soft stir
Air filled with fragrance nectar of myrrh

Oh beautiful tree I love you so much
I greet you each morning with loves tender touch
In autumns warm glow mine eyes do behold
Your wondrous form clothed in pure gold

***

Dancing Raindrops

Sparkling raindrops dancing in light
Shimmering twinkling in sunlight bright
A thousand rainbows dazzle and dance
I watch as I'm held in enchanted trance

The morning sun cascading light
Through whispering leaves awake from night
Caressed by water droplets lie
Glistening swaying with a sigh

Oh such wonder and beauty is found
In nature's glorious wondrous sound
Her fragrance lingers everywhere
Free as the wind for all to share

Her song sings out across the land
Listen reach and touch Her hand
Immerse in Her sound in your heart
Follow Her call that is flowing from Her loving heart

***

Living Earth

Living Earth gentle being
Quietly to your children seeing
Bringing forth abundant treasure
Wondrous beauty for man's pleasure

But man in darkness knows you not
He steals and plunders all you've got
With not a thought of causing pain
He brings pollution and acid rain

Savagely felling trees so tall
Crying weeping they do call
Stop this mindless senseless waste
In compassion please make haste

Replace the forests on this earth
And plant more trees to bring to birth
A new beginning of bright green woods
Or see all perish beneath the floods

Where Angels Sing

Give me thy hand where angels sing
Together we'll fly on golden wing
Forever as one, in Love we'll fly
Soaring through space we'll glide with a sigh

To rapturous heights above all things
Floating in Love on gossamer wings
High above earth our hearts joined as one
Enveloped in Love in radiant sun

Swirling in space
All around is His face
Free as The Dove
We swim in His Love

***

In The Silence Of The Night

In the silence of the night
Neath radiant stars that shine so bright
A wondrous baby boy was born
As that first Christmas Day did dawn

The creatures of the earth did know
In silent knowing they did go
Towards that Holy place where lies
A golden babe with gentle eyes

Learned men have seen the star
From far off lands have travelled far
To find the child of noble birth
Who'll show the way to those on earth

So find the star that still shines bright
Guiding men through darkest night
Look for the signs that show the way
To find once more where Christ doth lay

***

Christmas Cheer

Christmas cheer fills the air
The world is happy and gay
Smiling faces all around
Today is Christmas Day

A time of joy upon this earth
When love and peace prevail
When men and angels join in song
His glorious name to hail

Oh would this time forever stay
Dismissing war and greed
When men in peace together walk
And on His Love do feed

So put your hand in His on high
Let go of earthly fear
Have love and joy in all you do
Be full of Christmas cheer

A Gift of Love

Dancing swirling in the sands
Creating Light with loving hands
Singing dancing feathered friend
Precious gift with you I send

To that part of me I love
That lives and breathes in Holy Dove
Take this gift and give to her
Filled with frankincense and myrrh

Far away in distant land
Arrives a wondrous pure white band
Of gulls encircling in the skies
With heartfelt joy I lift mine eyes

They call my name and to me sing
A gift of love to me they bring
Such radiant Light from one I love
Who flies with me in Golden Dove

Two flames as one we'll always be
As we are both a part of He
In Love we fly two souls as one
In timelessness in golden sun

***

Sunset

Crimson gold and amber
Hues of God Divine
Look up unto the sunset
In radiance I do shine

My beauty I do share with you
Take time to realise
That all I have created
Is for you to feast your eyes

Stop your endless rushing
Slow down take time to be
Enjoy the countless Blessings
That emanate from Me

Life is meant to be enjoyed
A gift from Me to you
In Mother Nature lies the key
Have love in all you do

Appreciate the sunset
Appreciate the dawn
Appreciate all in between
For all from Me is born

You are all My children
Each one loved the same
Honour your Father and Mother
Heaven on Earth is found in My Name

"I Am Pure Love"

The Golden Apple

Food of the gods from sacred tree
A gift divine brought forth from She
Elixir sweet from Mother Earth
And Father God in sacred birth

Love and Wisdom merge as One
Creating light of golden sun
Daughters three as was as is
Joined in Love's eternal bliss

Priestesses pure in Father's Light
Sacred vows in sacred rites
The food of life is so divine
Nectar sweet and sacred wine

Sacred knowledge laws of old
Sisters three in love do hold
Eat their fruit and you will shine
Grow golden wings pure and fine

Held in love's pure trinity
Joined throughout infinity
Tapestry of light so pure
Forever one in love they soar

Emerge now from your chrysalis
Fly with them in loves pure bliss
Become the butterfly you are
And shine with love like golden star

***

Rainbow of Love

A rainbow of love appears in the sky
A sign from our God who watches on high
A symbol of Light radiant and bright
To lift all our hearts, such a pure wondrous sight

A link from the heavens touching the earth
A new year doth dawn bringing peace unto birth
Lift ye your spirits look up to the sky
In harmony walk with your heads held up high

Reach for the stars the universe is yours
The key is Pure Love to open its doors
A five-pointed star doth beckon the way
To heaven on earth in glorious array

***

Light of the World

On a night as still as a mill pond
A comet did herald the birth
Of The Son of God to a maiden pure
Who would touch all souls on this earth

Be still and remember most holy of nights
Just pause for a moment in time
With grateful heart thank God for His gift
And send love to His son divine

***

Peace in the Valley

Let peace be in the valley
The valley that's called Earth
To glorious global village
Our Father God gave birth

One sun doth shine in one sky
Warming all the land
Same river of life flowing
Pouring from God's hand

Same air we all breathe
As we journey through life
Same foods in abundance
From Our Mother, God's wife

Our Heavenly Father
Did create in great love
This heaven on earth
And doth watch from above

His children one family
The family of man
Conceived by Our Mother
In divine wondrous plan

Their children intended
To live by one law
Blessed and divine
In Pure Love were to soar

But man became greedy
And lost then his way
Forgetting his God
No longer did pray

In darkness he wandered
Cut off from The Source
Setting himself distant
Soon forgot sacred laws

Now is the time
To awake from dark night
Let God's sunlight shine
Golden and bright

Warming all hearts
With a peace that's divine
From slumber awake
And follow love's sign

Reach out to thy neighbour
In friendship and love
With joy in your heart
Lift your eyes up above

Paths there are many
The way it is love
To the same destination
Back home to Pure Dove

***

A Blessing

May the light of The Christ shine like a star
To guide your way home from near and far
May the love of The Christ glow like a sun
Guiding you home to The Heart of The One

Purfect Peace

A purfect start to a purfect year
To have someone you love nuzzle your ear
Such love we feel for one another
We're a very special sister and brother

Though different we be, well from outside in
Inside out we are both made of Him
Our skins are different our ways are too
But beneath the surface we're just like you

Our needs are the same, for love we all yearn
And whatever the name, 'tis to same God we all turn
For God gave us life and all that we need
In peace and in love on His gifts let's all feed

(This poem was written as a new year greeting, with an image of a puppy kissing a kitten's ear, but lends itself equally well to people too!)

***

Illusions

As above so below
Other worlds to you I'll show
A universe within a flower
A cosmic year within an hour

For time in truth does not exist
Eternity in loves sweet kiss
Illusions of mind mask the soul
A tiny seed contains the whole

The Universe in a grain of sand
Created by The Divine Hand
Far more exists than eye can see
The vastness of space lies within you and me

***

I Am Always Near

Just to say I love you
More than you do know
You're in my heart you're in my soul
Wherever you do go

My love is with you constantly
With arms of love surround
I whisper words of love to you
In forms of sacred sound

And even when you feel alone
Or feeling down or blue
My love is there for you to hold
Reach out I'm close to you

For nought can break the bonds of love
Blessed by God Divine
Through darkest clouds in golden hue
Gold rays of love do shine

So next time you feel lonely
Despondent, lost, in fear
Just call my name within your heart
For I am always near

Guardian of The Earth

Gentle angel Gaia
Guardian of the Earth
All God's creatures know her
Brought forth in divine birth

One with Earthly Mother
Blessed by God above
Her Heavenly Father watches
In form of Holy Dove

Blessings to all nature
In her loving touch
Gentle heart in purity
Doth love the Earth so much

Hear her gentle lullaby
Floating on the breeze
Filled with loving whispers
Echoes in the trees

The Heart of God in nature
In purity is found
Be still and quietly listen
To His sacred sound

All His wondrous visions
In majesty behold
Creation all around us
In shades of green untold

Those who love God's creatures
And love to them are giving
Those who rejoice in nature
Close to God are living

Kiss of Love

A kiss of love to divine child of light
Its radiance cascading like jewels in the night
The heartbeat of God doth echo within
His son now is born to take away sin

The sound of his heart gently beats with God's love
To Mary was given the seed of The Dove
Be still now and listen and capture the sound
In harmony of light his essence is found

Breathe in his fragrance, his fragrance divine
Ask for the way and follow the sign
His love still lives on and is waiting to share
In wondrous bliss that nought else can compare

Open your heart to sweet rhapsody of love
Capture love's droplets that cascade from above
A fountain of light doth pour forth from The Source
Bathe in its essence that teams with life force

The comet announced the saviour's birth
A child born to raise man from bondage on earth
To bring man to know the spirit divine
To let go of fear, let love's inner light shine

His spirit lives on and is calling to thee
Take hold of my hand and set thyselves free
For love is the way that all men must take
From long dark filled days 'tis now time to awake

This time was foretold by the prophets of old
A new dawn will break in ambers and gold
But first we must sort the chaff from the wheat
And gather the harvest, in love we must meet

And then only then will paradise return
'tis love pure sweet love that all souls do yearn
So reach out to Love with a heart that's sincere
Let Love take your hand and dismiss all your fear

Call out Love's name from the depths of your soul
The Divine Hand of God your tears will console
With Love in your heart go forward in might
To save God's Creation and return all to Light

***

Festival of Light

The Festival of Light is once more here
When angel beings gather near
To honour one who came to earth
In sacredness of divine birth

The Way of Love he taught to all
His voice still echoes with Love's call
Be still and look into the sky
See angel beings flying by

Few remember the essence of love
Why angels do gather in heaven above
They immerse themselves in treasures of earth
Instead of remembering The Saviour's birth

So spare a few moments amidst all the din
Remember the child who was born of Him
Remember the gift of life that he brought
And The Way of Love that he always taught

His spirit lives on in the hearts of a few
And longs for the time when peace comes into view
When all men will return to know Love Divine
And bathe in the fountain of life that doth shine

So gather now all those of The Light
Celebrate in wonder and awe this night
Immerse in love and sing loves sweet song
And join in praise with angelic throng

***

Winters Chill

Winters chill is in the air
A time of peace for all to share
Resting now is Mother Earth
She slumbers deep before rebirth

Her treasures shared abundantly
For all our food doth come from She
Pause a while in gratitude
For all the gifts She has imbued

Nurture gently Mother's breast
As She lays in sleep and rest
For we of Her are given life
She is Our Father's Sacred Wife

Our Earthly Mother and Father Divine
Entwined as One in Love do shine
She receives pure seed of He
We live and breath brought forth from She

Love Is All

Precious friend I love you so
Always there where're I go
I love to feel you by my side
My deepest thoughts in you confide

Of my life you are a part
Held so close within my heart
We share such joy and purest love
That flows so freely from above

When sometimes far you have to go
My love goes with you this you know
For love is all there is it's true
It bathes us both in wondrous hue

I miss you so when we're apart
An empty space doth touch my heart
Until the time when you return
When once again to you I turn

Then once more I feel complete
As in Pure Love our spirit's meet
In such bliss on Love we feed
For Love is all the food we need

***

Sacred Wine

On nectar sweet thy spirit feed
The sacred table's set
Love divine is all you need
Thy spirit's wishes met

Take a sip of sacred wine
Nought else can e'er compare
In radiance bright your soul will shine
As food of love we share

The cares of earth will fade away
As nourishment you take
Complete in Love as one we lay
Forever and a day

***

Touched by Love

Soft gentle rain
Falling from the sky
Touch the earth with love
Wherever you may lie

Breezes whisper softly
Tender words of love
Carried on the outstretched wings
Of radiant Holy Dove

Golden sun bring forth thy warmth
Caressing earth so pure
Nourished by sweet rays of love
New life from her will pour

All will be renewed in Love
The Source of All that Is
Paradise will be restored
And all will know Love's bliss

Nature's New Year

Nature's new year
Is already here
From long dark night
She awakens to light

Gently unfolding
Her beauty soon showing
Goddess divine
With Love She doth shine

Born in such splendour
To Love doth surrender
In constant rebirth
Lives gentle sweet Earth

In honour of One
She is warmed by the sun
Pure water doth feed
Her sacred new seed

***

Nesting Time

All around birds nests I see
There's one in each and every tree
Sounds of joy do fill the air
The songs of birds for all to share

There's blackbirds on the right hand side
And on the left sweet doves do hide
Starlings whizzing to and fro
Such a delight is nature's show

And Betsy stands in fine array
Conducting traffic every way
From the north the ravens come
And land in light of morning sun

Seagulls too fly overhead
As hedgehogs wake from winters bed
Magpies also join the dance
As on my lawn they all do prance

Bumblebees are now awake
And from each flower sweet nectar take
Paradise right here on earth
As Mother Nature doth give birth

Reborn anew in wondrous hue
A gift divine for me and you
My heart and soul are filled with love
To see such gifts from Holy Dove

(*'Betsy' is a beautiful big apple tree*)

***

Love's Sweet Trance

Hypnotized in love's sweet trance
My heart and soul with thee do dance
Amongst the stars in love we fly
Eternity within a sigh

Soul Sounds

My soul doth speak in sacred sounds
Notes of love that echo around
No words are needed only pure love
That flows through me from Holy Dove

His voice doth whisper in my soul
Words of Love that do console
A melody floats on the breeze
Whispering through Mother's trees

Time stands still in rhapsody
Symphonic sounds and poetry
My Love doth speak within pure thought
In sound and rhyme His essence brought

I share His Love in every note
As from my spirit they do float
Uplifting those who seek Pure Love
Touching all hearts with Mother's Love

***

Love In Abundance

My cup runneth over with Love from The Source
I share its abundance as through me it pours
Drink from the chalice and know Love Divine
Sip Love's sweet nectar of heavenly wine

In Loving Hands

The earth is held in loving hands
Oceans, trees, rivers, sands
From Her pain She'll be reborn
All renewed one golden dawn

Purest Love doth cradle Her
As in Her womb birth pangs stir
From seeds of Love sweet blossoms new
Rebirth and joy in golden hue

***

The Joy of Love

The joy of Love doth fill me so
His presence pure I do know
He fills my soul with Love Divine
He feeds my spirit sacred wine

Nought can compare to my Pure Love
My wondrous radiant Holy Dove
I call His name in silence loud
I float in Love on golden cloud

My body His in all I do
My heart and soul and spirit too
I give myself to Love Divine
In Love returned pure gold I shine

***

Complete in Love

In Purest Love their spirits meet
Merged as one they are complete
No thoughts of earth just Love Divine
In joy and bliss they intertwine

Dancing 'midst the stars so bright
Hand in hand in wondrous Light
Father Sun and Mother Earth
As was, as is, in constant rebirth

***

Midnight Glow

In silence filled with Love I rest
In golden robes I now am dressed
The food of life is so divine
I take my fill of sacred wine

Content once more in Love complete
His Holy Spirit I did greet
He feeds my body heart and soul
Such nectar sweet in me I hold

My temple filled with divine seed
The food of life is all I need
Without His Love I'd surely die
I rest in peace my soul doth fly

***

Mountain Stream

Mountain stream tumbling falling
Pine laden air eagles calling
Down through the forests swiftly darting
Rocks and stones shifting parting

Onwards onwards crystal streaming
Sunlight shining dancing beaming
Meadows fields cowbells ringing
Buttercups growing blackbirds singing

Valleys below resplendent in green
Waterfowl nesting soon to be seen
Fishes swimming bodies shining
Frogs and toads herons dining

Slowing now quietly flowing
From the source to ocean going
Weeping willows gently swaying
Ducks and geese laughing playing

Majestic swans graceful gliding
Chicks and cygnets running hiding
Widening now fishing boats tied
Down to the sea gently we glide

Salt in the air journey ending
Nearing the ocean gently bending
From stream to river to ocean flowing
Unending cycle of life showing

***

The Breath of Life

She walked alone without a sound
When there beside the path she found
A gentle creature now no more
Lying still upon the floor

No breath did flow through body frail
Its head lay still upon its tail
Its pretty form an empty case
No life in such a pretty face

She reached to it with hands of love
Oh precious fragile gentle dove
She breathed on it with spirit pure
And gave it life once more to soar

And fly again with body new
Its spirit free returns anew
For love gives life and with it brings
The power to fly on golden wings

***

White Lace

Delicate snowflakes fall from the sky
Crystals of ice quietly lie
Gently caressing trees growing tall
Covering the ground with lace as they fall
In silent splendour for all to see
Showing God's beauty to you and me

Out of the Darkness

Out of the darkness sunlight is born
Casting its light to herald the dawn
Awaken from slumber look now and see
His radiant light now is shining on thee

Oh wondrous orb of golden light
Piercing the darkest shadows of night
Shining so bright in amber array
Lifting our spirits this glorious day

For dark can't exist in the presence of light
Such vibrance and radiance dismisses from sight
All that is not a part of God's plan
To bring now once more new life unto man

Life of the spirit still sleeping in most
Till wakened once more by angelic host
So rise and emerge from out of the dark
And dance in the sun and sing with the lark

***

Words of Love

He came to me my love once more
My hearts delight my soul did soar
His arms outstretched in Love did greet
In wondrous Love our eyes did meet

Words of love He spoke to me
My eyes in tears His form did see
No words can say the love I know
My Father God I love Thee so

One Endless Moment

Time in essence does not exist
Nature by The Hand of God is kissed
Constantly breathing out and then in
Life giving pulses flowing from Him

One endless moment no beginning or end
Spiralling upwards to heaven we wend
Waking then sleeping cradled in Light
Held in His arms radiant and bright

***

Jewels of Love

Jewels of love sparkle and glisten
To the songs of birds be still and listen
Raindrops glow in radiant light
Oh what a glorious wondrous sight

My heart is filled with love so pure
To see His beauty my soul doth soar
I see His presence all around
As nature's song of love doth sound

The sun shines down upon the earth
She sighs with love and brings to birth
Another wondrous bright new morn
In glorious robes she greets the dawn

***

Journeys End

Floating slowly back to earth
From deepest space in joyous birth
In Love like nought I'd known before
In His Light my soul did soar

My spirit touched the brightest star
My soul in joy did travel far
I then returned reborn renewed
Nourished by sweet sacred food

***

Golden River

Father God my Lord Divine
I share with Thee Thy sacred wine
I bathe in bliss in waters pure
That flows from golden temple door

Immersed in Love I float and swim
In joy and bliss I bathe with Him
My spirit free and flying high
Content in Love I breathe a sigh

Once more refreshed fulfilled anew
Glistening now in golden hue
Golden River I now leave
Its essence into sound I weave

***

Inspiration

Inspiration flows from He
Inspiration flows through me
His gentle voice within I hear
Breathes words of love into my ear

His words I then transmute to sound
His love in every note is found
Be still and listen to my love
My radiant pure white Holy Dove

***

If Music be the Food of Love

If music be the food of love
Then let me feed some more
It feeds and nourishes heart and soul
And lets my spirit soar

I fly in wondrous golden hue
With radiant angels bright
I sing and dance in love so pure
In robes of vibrant light

Rainbows divine encircle me
As in His breath I dance
Intoxicating fragrance pure
Doth hold me in a trance

Of love beyond all knowledge
Earth lost in time and space
Merged as one with Love itself
I gaze upon His face